THE
Favor

Marche' Scott

Copyright © 2021 by Marche' Scott

All rights reserved. No part of this publication may be reproduced, distributed, or transmitted in any form or by any means, including photocopying, recording, or other electronic or mechanical methods, without the prior written permission of the author, except in the case of brief quotations embodied in critical reviews and certain other noncommercial uses permitted by copyright law.

ISBN: 978-1-64314-703-1 (Paperback)
       978-1-64314-704-8 (Hardback)
       978-1-64314-705-5 (E-book)

AuthorsPress
California, USA
www.authorspress.com

DEDICATION

I want to dedicate this book to my darling daughter,

Semira! Mommie loves you with every inch of my being!

CONTENTS

ACKNOWLEDGMENTS vii

1 Baby Girl 1

2 The Unknown 33

3 Prey 63

4 Road Blocks 99

5 Entangled 121

6 The Blame Game 159

7 Fight Back 175

8 New Beginnings 201

ABOUT THE AUTHOR 229

ACKNOWLEDGMENTS

I want to thank The Lord for birthing this book through me. It was a rocky rollercoaster to the finish; however, nothing is too big or too small for my God to handle.

Baby Girl

"Auntie, I'm so excited to be moving into my first apartment," Chanel chimed as her grandmother listened over the phone.

"I told you, baby, God got you! He's going to carry you through. When you put God first in everything you do, he will carry you and do the rest."

"I know, Auntie," Chanel replied, annoyed as she rolled her eyes. "Well, I should start unpacking and getting settled."

"Okay baby, I love you, and I'm so proud of you," Chanel grandmother replied

"Love you too, auntie, bye!"

"Bye, baby"…Chanel hung up the phone and instantly felt the loneliness, and it echoed coldly throughout her apartment walls. Chanel was a young 19-year-old college student attending the University of Philadelphia. She was a senior and majored in Biochemistry, with a bright future ahead of her. She was part of a sorority; she had a lucrative business selling weave, which aided her in paying for school, participated in tons of charity events that served youth living in poverty, and an activist. But, there was one thing missing. Chanel longed for a life partner. She wasn't much of a clubber and spent most of her time working on her business, school, and sorority. She was increadibly lonely. She longed for the touch of a man. Her last boyfriend was in high-school, and she quickly left him once she became a college freshman.

"Uh… let me start unpacking," she moaned. She didn't have a lot of stuff, so unpacking would be easy for her. So she proceeded to deep clean both her new kitchen and bathroom. A habit she learned from her grandmother, "I don't know who's been in here. I want to make sure it's clean before I put my stuff up"… After cleaning, Chanel designed her bathroom in navy and bright yellow accented with gold. She hung a beautiful shower curtain that depicted a lighthouse on a shore colored in navy and white and accents of gold. On her sink, she placed a gold mosaic vase filled with fake flowers; on her walls were paintings of contemporary lines in soft yellow art.

"This is coming together nicely,"… she said to herself. She admired the work she did.

"Hmmm… Should I do my kitchen or paint the town?"… As much as she wanted to organize her kitchen, she also wanted a break. In the hallway outside her door, she heard a loud slam.

"Ole funky a** b*****," she heard a man groan. *"Whose that?"* She thought to herself. Chanel peeped through her peephole and caught a glimpse of a younger man right before he walked up the steps to the second level of the condo complex. She heard him slam his door shut. *"hmm"*… Chanel ran to the living room window to see if anyone was there. Outside was an older woman who walked real 'stank back to her building. Chanel watched this woman from her window

"F*** you too, you wack a** n****. That's why everybody knows yo d*** is little… B****!" she retorted as she stomped back to her apartment condo, slamming the door behind herself.

"Well, some neighbors!" Chanel thought. She couldn't wait until she spoke with her Aunt again to talk about her new neighbors. "Back to more important matters," as she once again deliberated on whether or not to continue with unpacking and to set up the kitchen or calling it a night and hanging out with a few friends. Chanel opted for painting the town for a few hours, *"a mini celebration with my girl wouldn't hurt."* Chanel grabbed her phone and texted Courtney,

"Hey girl, you wanna hang out for a few hours?" she waited for her reply.

"That doesn't sound like a bad idea. What did you have in mind?" Courtney asked through the message.

"Hmmm. What about Asian Persuasion? I'm in the mood for Asian tacos."

"Yes!!! Hell yes!"

"Bet! Wanna meet up at 5:30"

"That sounds good. I'm finna hop in the shower, and I'll meet you there". Yes! The perfection distraction from doing housework. She laid on her bare mattress that sat on her bedroom on the floor. *I can't believe that I finally have my own condo.* Chanel was so excited about what her future held. "Everything is coming together so nicely," she thought to herself and dozed off.

"Oh crap, I hope it didn't oversleep" Chanel glanced down at her apple watch, and the time read 5:10 pm.

"Let me hurry up!" She ran to her bathroom and freshened up. She dressed in a black mini dress with silver buttons on the backside, her black sandals with the thick strap over the foot, and huge silver studs that bedazzled in her ear. She lightly coated her face with a neutral deep ebony shade bronzer, a soft silver eye shadow, and black eyeliner that accented her deep brown mahogany eyes, and a brownish-red matt lip! She fluffed her afro with a spray bottle misting the olive oil and water all over kinky coils. She glanced at herself once in the mirror, "damn, I look good!" Chanel grabbed her purse, keys, and wallet as she motioned towards the door. She took one glance over her shoulder to admire her new condo!

She stepped out in the hallway and turned to lock her door. She felt her heart flutter as it started to sink in that she was doing exceptionally well for herself at the age of 19. As Chanel motioned to walk out of the building, she noticed someone was blocking the door.

"Excuse me," she spoke softly. The younger gentleman turned around, and Chanel found herself instantly attracted to him. He looked to be 5'7, 150 lbs., solid build, light, and braids to the back. She eyed him from a distance... *"whose that?"* she wondered. Chanel marveled over him. *"He's fine."* She was so focused on him; she didn't realize she was staring hard. She looked up from her trance and saw he was staring right back at her.

"How you were doing?" he spoke with a wide grin.

Chanel, realizing that he was on to her, changed her attitude. She went from nice to bitchy in .5 seconds.

"Hey," she said back, kind of stank.

He frowned and gave her a smudge look in return.

Chanel caught notice and quickly opened the door to leave her building and brushed it off.

"UHHH, I hate when they do that," she mumbled to herself. But deep down, she wanted to get to know him better. Maybe some other time.

She hopped into her custom yellow mini cooper and adjusted herself in the mirror one last time before she drove off to meet her friend. She glanced down at the clock, "5:35 pm. Welp, I'll be a little late; I'll just shot her a text and let her know". She arrived around 5:50 pm and found close parking near the restaurant. Inside Asian Persuasion, she found Courtney sitting near the back of the restaurant texting on her phone.

"Hey girl," Chanel said as she approached.

"Dang, about time… lol, hey boo," Courtney teased as she reached and hugged Chanel from across the table.

"I know, girl, and I dozed off by mistake," Chanel replied as she returned the embrace and took her seat across from her.

"So congrats!!!," Courtney exclaimed as she handed Chanel a drink.

"Thank you, girl," Chanel beamed back, taking a small sip of her drink. "I'm just truly blessed, honestly! God has been showing out."

"Girl, I'm next in line for my blessing."

"Sis, he got you next! Speak it into existence."

"Girl, I'm already claiming it. So give me details about the new place?"

"Yes, it's a one-bedroom condo, open concept of course with living room and kitchen, a bathroom with an insanely huge shower head, nice size room, bedroom massive, carpet in the bedroom, hardwood floors in the kitchen and living room, a walkout patio, vaulted ceilings, rounded countertops in the kitchen, detachable showerhead."

"YASSSS SIS"

"Yea girl, I'm just happy."

A waiter approached their table, "Hello ladies, my name is Ty, and I will be your server this evening. Can I a start you off with some drinks?"

"Yes, can I get another strawberry-passion fruit fusion, please?" Courtney requested.

"Yes, ma'am," the waiter took Courtney's order. "Anything for you, ma'am?" The waiter asked Chanel.

"Yes, can I order a kiwi splash cherry limeade?"

"Yes, ma'am, I'll be back with your drinks shortly." The waiter walked away and put in their drink orders.

"Girl, why my neighbors got into it today."

"Dang, already? At least let settle in before they start acting up," They both laughed.

"Right! The upstairs from me called her a b****, and the woman said his d*** was little real loud outside where everybody can hear."

Courtney choked on her drink, "For real? OMG, I can tell your spot is about to get juicy because HUNTY summer is right around the corner, and you know your cousins don't know how to act when it gets warm outside."

"Girl, now, them your cousins, and they cutting up already in these spring months." Both ladies laughed in unison.

"So?" Courtney asked, "got anyone special in your life?"

"No, not really," Chanel replied. For some odd reason, her neighbor popped back into her mind. She quickly erased the thought of him and continued her evening with Courtney. The waitress returned and took their orders. Both ladies enjoyed each other company. They caught each other up on everything that was presently going on in each of their lives: the good, the bad, and the ugly. The ladies lost track of time and didn't realize how late it was.

"Girl, we've been sitting here for hours. What time this place close. I know they are tired of us!" Chanel said in a joking manner

"Girl, who you are telling!" Courtney replied. Chanel looked down at her watch and saw it was 9:00 pm.

"Girl, it's 9!"

"Ooh, let's get our tails out of here, honey. I didn't know it was that late" Both ladies paid for their meals and walked to their cars.

"It was nice seeing you, girl. I truly enjoyed your company. We should do this more often," Courtney said as she was entering her vehicle.

"Yes, we shall. It was nice seeing you too," Chanel replied. Chanel got into her car and drove away. She turned the radio on and let the smooth sounds of Jill Scott fill her car.

"Is it the waaaay, you lovvvveeee, me babbbby" She sang along. Just then, her mind flashed to her neighbor again.

"Oh my gosh," she spoke in disgust to herself, "why do I keep thinking of him?" As before, she quickly shook the thought of him out of her mind. She continued her car ride home in silence. She was embarrassed by her behavior. She felt it was better not to further listen to Jill Scott. Chanel arrived home around 9:30 pm.

"Back at last," she said to herself. She exited her car and chirped the lock. As she got ready to enter the building, she saw a man standing in the hallway through the outer glass door. Proceeding with caution, as she entered, she realized it was her neighbor standing in the hallway drinking a beer. She immediately turned red. She remembered how she briefly thought about him during dinner and on the car ride home. He turned around and saw her standing there. Being friendly, he gestured a wave and smiled in her direction. In return, Chanel ignored his gesture and made her way right to her door without so much of an acknowledgment.

"Well, excuse me," he said, in a deep un-thrilled voice. Chanel felt herself become hot.

"Ohh, sorry. Hi," she said in an unamused way. She opened her door and let herself in. As she turned to close the door, she saw him staring at her. She quickly closed it and took a deep breath.

"ugh," she breathed! Chanel couldn't figure out why she reacted the way she did. I mean, it's not like he did anything to her. All he said was hi.

"I suppose I can be nicer. Maybe tomorrow." She thought to herself. Chanel got ready for bed. She took another shower and slid into her favorite pj's from Victoria secret. She set her alarm to 7:30 a.m. and proceeded to get some shut-eye.

The next morning, Chanel's alarm awakened her. "Aye, good ole 7:30". She arose from her bed, still slightly sleepy, and made her way to the bathroom for her morning ritual. Her usual, using the restroom and strolling social media for 5-10 minutes while sitting on the toilet. She will eventually get up, wash her hands and brush her teeth, start her morning coffee, pick her clothes out for the day, do her makeup, style her hair, put on her clothes, and pour herself a cup of morning joe before grabbing her keys and purse to head out the door. She glanced down at her watch; it read 8:15 a.m. Perfect timing. Her class didn't start until 8:45 a.m., and she lived less than 15 minutes away from school. Out the gate she was. She locked up behind her and headed for the outer door that leads to her car. As she made her way down the steps, she saw a man standing outside with his earphones. *"dang is that my neighbor…"* she thought to herself. *"Okay, girl gets yourself together; you got this!"* Too late! He spotted her. But to her surprise, he held open the door for her.

"Thank you and good morning," she spoke.

"Good morning," he replied. Chanel quickly glanced him over. He had on workout clothes. Basketball shorts, no shirt that showed his tattoos up and down his arms and body, and pretty fair completed skin. He had the smoothest skin she's ever seen. She felt herself get turned on at the sight of him. *"Control yourself, girl. You barely know him. Relax!"* Chanel laughed it off and walked to her car. As she was walking away, her neighbor said

"Did I do something to you yesterday?"

"No," Chanel replied nervously.

"Well, why did you make that face at me?"

"I'm sorry, I was in deep thought about something else."

"You sure? It seems intentional."

"Yes, I'm positive."

"Aw, okay." She walked a little further to her car and, "you got a man?"

"No"

"Awh, that's why you act like that."

"Act like what?"

"All stank."

"That's rude."

"Just like how you were rude to me yesterday?" At this point, Chanel was annoyed with this conversation, plus it was honestly intervening with her time.

"I would love to sit and chat, but I have somewhere I have to be," she said in a firm tone. He threw his hands up in a "defensive way" and shook his head. Chanel got into her car and drove away, frustrated. *Who the hell does he think he is talking to me like that? Do I have a man? That's none of his business.* Chanel drove in utter silence on the way to school. She kept replaying the conversation over and over again in her mind. When she pulled up in front of the building, she was so involved with her thoughts, she almost hit a pedestrian.

"Omg, I'm sorry," Chanel mouthed to the young college student standing in the street. *"Get yourself together girl."* She quickly prayed to the Lord for a productive class day. She gathered her things, locked the car, and entered the building. As Chanel made her way to room 1E, a classmate stopped her.

"Hey girl."

"Hey"

"How are you? Are you okay? You looked stressed," her classmate asked inquisitively. Oh crap!

"Yes, girl, I'm doing good!" Chanel replied. Not wanting to reveal the altercation she had with her neighbor moments prior.

"Did you finish that chem quiz online?"

"Yes, I got 87%. How did you do?"

"Gurl, I got a 67%."

"Girl, you should have called me. I definitely would have helped."

"I'll remember that next time."

"Let's go in and get our seats. Class is about to start, and you know that Mrs. Fuero does not play about being late."

"Girl, yes, we don't want to upset her." Both ladies made their way into the classroom and found a seat near the front. Mrs. Fuero had an olive complexion with sandy brown hair with grays here and there. Her eyes were narrow, and her nose was long and slender. She wore her glasses down on her nose the majority of the time and rarely readjusted them. She was tall but had a small frame. Her voice was a bit nasally. She reminded Chanel of Fran fine when she spoke.

"Good morning class," Mrs. Fuero spoke.

"Good morning," the class said in unison. "How was the chemistry homework over chapter 5? Did any of you have any difficulty?" Some of the students nodded their heads. Mrs. Fuero asked those specific students which questions gave them the most trouble. As Mrs. Fuero continued with her lesson of going over the Chem quiz, Chanel found herself thinking about her neighbor. *Maybe I can be nicer to him. That wouldn't hurt. After all, I am the mean one.* Chanel could hardly pay attention in class because her mind kept drifting back to her neighbor. She was so wrapped up in her own thoughts. She did hear Mrs. Fuero directly ask her a question.

"Ms. Woodson," Mrs. Fuero said again.

"Oh, I'm sorry," Chanel replied, embarrassed.

"Are you okay?"

"Yes, I'm fine."

"Did you have any problems with the homework?"

"No ma'am."

"Okay, good. Stop day-dreaming, please, and pay attention."

"Yes, ma'am." Chanel sunk into her chair. *I need to get myself together!* Chanel made a full effort to ignore her thoughts about her neighbor and focus in her chem class. After chem class was over, Chanel hurried out of the room and rushed to her car. She a meeting with a customer about some of the hair that was bought off her site. Chanel decided to get a quick bite to eat before heading to the forum. She stopped at a Mcdonald's and ordered a spicy Mcchicken sandwich, a small fry, and water. She pulled through the drive-through and paid her money. As she waited for her food, her phone ring, it was the customer.

"Hello," Chanel answered.

"Hey girl, are we still on for our meeting?"

"Yes, ma'am, I have you down for 10:30 this morning."

"Awesome!"

"Okay, I'll be over at yours in a few."

"Alright, that sounds good. See you in a few". Chanel hung up the phone. She looked over and saw the attendant was waiting on her.

"I'm sorry," Chanel said as she rolled down her window to retrieve her food.

"It's alright."

"Thank you, and have a nice day." Chanel pulled off while sticking a hot French fry in her mouth. Chanel pulled in front of her client's house within 10 minutes, eating her food on the way. *Let me chew some gum right quick.* She popped winter fresh spearmint gum into her mouth to freshen' up her breath. *You can't be blowing stank breath in their face.* Chanel parked her car, groomed herself in the mirror once more, and adjusted her Louis Vuitton belt where her Gucci button-down fit snugly into her black jeans. Chanel gathered her keys, purse, and ray ban sunglasses and exited the car. She made her way to the trunk, to retrieve the sample bundles so that her client can feel the texture of each set. As Chanel closed her box her client was already standing in the doorway waiting for her.

"Hey, Chanel girl," her client said.

"Hey," Chanel replied, "are you ready to be wonder, weave-able?" Both ladies laughed in unison. Chanel walked into her client's home and waited for her to motion which direction they would be sitting in.

"Please follow me," the client said as she led Chanel down a hallway into a small yellow and teal kitchen. "You can set-up right here," the client motioned towards the kitchen table.

"Thanks," Chanel placed all the products on the table and waited until her client was seated.

"How are things going?" Chanel asked. She always aimed for client satisfaction by asking about their day, livelihood, whatever that will keep the money rolling in. Not that she didn't care about her clients, but this is business.

"Everything is going fine. No complaints. I can't wait for my trip in two weeks to the Dominican".

"ooh, that sounds lovely."

"Yes, girl, that's why I'm having you come over. So I can get this head together before I leave for my trip. I want to be wonder weave-able hunty!" Both ladies laughed hysterically.

"Okay, boo, I got you. So today, I brought some of my finest hair that will deliver what you are looking for. I remembered our last conversation, and you stated you wanted hair full of body, bounce, and volume. You also stated you wanted hair wavy with a deep curl and reacted to water for a more exotic look. Well, I present to you today 3 of my best pieces that I'm sure will satisfy your hair needs". Chanel was a beast. She learns all of her clients and provides nothing but the best. After they fill out the online questionnaire, she searches high and low for the right hair that meets every client's need, and pays her big bucks for it! This hair is not for the cheap. She is serious about her money, and all her clients know, that when they shop with her, you better be talking big cash! Chanel grabbed the first wig from her bag. It came in a silk pink bedazzled bag with the words Luxury Aesthetics printed boldly across the front. The bag was drawstring. Inside the bag was the wig secured within another cloth-like bag. She opened both bags and pulled out a 30 in' Glamorous Wavy Deep Spiral Curl lace front wig. Chanel looked over to her client to decipher her facial expression. The client's eyes widened with excitement. *YES!*

"This is was a hard find. This Glamorous Wavy Deep Spiral Curl lace front is a dream come true! This lace front wig is a must-have and will compliment your beautiful round face. It provides a voluptuous body and definition. Imagine yourself in this wig, and all eyes will turn in your direction. Girl, you will steal the runway with this wig! Might I add, it is extremely soft to touch made from 100% human hair and last for a very long time?" Chanel extended the wig over to her client to let her feel the texture of the hair.

"Ohh, this feels nice. I like this. How much?"

"Asking price is $450."

"Mhm, not bad,"... her client was impressed. "okay, what else do you have?" Chanel reached into her bag and pulled out a second pink bedazzled Luxury Aesthetic bag. She removed the second cloth bag containing the hair. She then pulled out a 29 in' Bossy Drip Wave Lace Front Wig. "This wig screams top-notch chick with all the attitude to make his new chick sick. This beauty is a top seller with all of my other clients. Just about everyone loves this wig. It's very natural in flare and style and adds a layer of sophistication to any look you're going for. Walk-in confidence wearing this wig around town. You will turn heads." Chanel glanced up from her demonstration to discern her client's face. This time, the client wore a blank expression. *Mhmm*. Testing the waters, "would you like to touch the wig?" Chanel offered.

"Uhm, I suppose,"... the client extended her hands to review the wig. She looked it over a few times unamused. "How much?"

"$350," Chanel replied. Chanel could instantly tell the client was not interested in that particular wig. "I have one more," Chanel responded in full confidence.

"Okay," the client replied happily, "let's see it."

"Okay, the moment we've all been waiting for. The top finale wig! This beauty is like drinking the most expensive wine known to man. It will quench the thirst of all who sees her. She demands attention. She is sexy. Delicious. Mysterious. Charming. Flirty. Expensive to all that wants to drink from her ever-flowing fountain. No man or woman will resist you after being seen in such a beautiful wig." Chanel looked over at her client and noticed she was all ears. Chanel pulled out her last pink bedazzled Luxury Aesthetic bag that housed the final wig. She continued with her presentation as she pulled the hair from its cloth bag. "This wig is literally to die for. Just imagine how many men will drop to your feet after seeing you in such an illuminating hairpiece. I present to you my 32 in' Italian Classy Loose Body Wave lace front." Chanel removed the wig from its bag and held it high so that her client can drool over it.

"OOOH," the client exhaled! "That's beautiful!" *Gotcha!* Chanel whispered to herself.

"Can I touch it?" her client asked as she reached over to retrieve the wig.

"Yes!" Chanel replied excitedly.

"This wig is beautiful and soft! Oh, my goodness. This is exactly what I've been looking for! It has the perfect curl, and I can imagine how many heads I will turn in this bad boy! How much?"

"$550," Chanel replied. The client got quiet. Chanel studied her face. Poker face she was. Then finally, "you got yourself a deal!"

"Excellent. How would you be paying?"

"Card"

"Awesome, I have my card swipe with me." Chanel pulled out the card swipe and attached it to her phone. The client left the room to retrieve her purse. I came back and purchased the wig.

"Pleasure doing business by you!" Chanel replied happily.

"Yes, Pleasure doing business with you too." Chanel wrapped her presentation with providing hair care tips, business cards, and a calendar of scheduled events where she will be a vendor. Chanel gathered her things and headed towards the door. "Thank you once again for doing business with me."

"Absolutely. I will be doing business with you again!" the client replied. The client opened the door and let Chanel out. *"Another day another dollar,"* Chanel mumbled to herself as she walked to her car. She felt invincible. Chanel is always proud of her work as a young entrepreneur. She works extremely hard for her money. It's also how she pays her way through college. She started her hair business sophomore year after participating in the Alpha Phi Alpha Miss Black and Gold pageant. She expressed to the judges she wanted to be an influential entrepreneur and own a business before she graduating college. And boom, Luxury Aesthetics was born. Since then, she has been making residual income, and all her clients refer to potential clients. Chanel was about her A-game! Just about anything she set out to do, she manifests it. To be only 19 years old is truly a blessing in her eyes. She wants to become a millionaire by 30!

Chanel got in her car and rode home for an afternoon nap before heading to the library to do school work. On her way home, all she thought about was her future and the life she hoped to live. She grew up in poverty and didn't want that for herself. She didn't have a great relationship with her mother or her father. Her mother was a hardworking woman. She did the best that she could. Their relationship was not the best. She put Chanel out at the age of 16. She felt she was too "grown." They would fight over things like chores, rules, homework, boys, etc. Chanel just had enough of it. She was tired. Chanel didn't feel like she had a life living at home with her mother. She felt like her mother was too hard on her. Her father, on the other hand, barely saw him. He was barely there. Frequently in and out of her life. A job here, a job there, fired or quit. In his later years, he got on drugs really bad. He was found dead in an alley from a drug overdose a few months back. She had other siblings by her father; she didn't really reach out to them as much. She honestly felt foreign to them. Her aunt practically raised her and did the best she could supporting her. Chanel was extremely grateful for her aunt and wanted to pay her back for pouring into her all these years. She tried to spend her mother back too! Even though they didn't have the best relationship, Chanel still loved her mother very much! She also recognized her mother did the best she could at raising her. Chanel wanted to make amends with her mother and make things right. She hasn't spoken to her since she left. "One day," she said to herself.

Chanel's life was somewhat complicated. Besides dealing with her father's death, her broken relationship with her mother, she was dealing with a deep internal battle with herself. Chanel battled suicide, and depression constantly. She wanted help but was afraid to ask. To make matters worse, she was a rape survivor and no one in her family knew. She felt shame if she was to tell them that she was raped. The voices in her head would automatically tell her she's guilty, and it's her fault. It's her fault she was raped. She should have been wiser, she should have been smarter, she should have fought back harder. The more she replayed the rape in her head, the more she felt shame to tell anyone.

"What would people think of me?" she wondered out loud to herself. Chanel was not the "type" to get raped. People viewed her as strong, determined, outspoken, smart, and wise. She was not the type to take s*** from anyone. It was unlike her to be in a predicament like that. Chanel thought that women who were raped were women who could quickly get taken advantage of. Women who didn't realize their worth and so unknowingly attract negative energy men who also didn't find these women worthy and do to them as they wished. That view of rape came crashing down when she became the very thing she talked about. Never in a million years did Chanel ever believe she would be a rape victim. What's more, triggering is that she hid it to herself. She never spoke of it.

The rape altered Chanel and her view of self. Mixing rape with depression and suicidal tendencies is a horrible combination. She began to hate herself, self-loath, self-pity, anger, bitterness, fear, depression, anxiety, PTSD, and an altered self-view. She didn't find herself worthy anymore. The mighty Chanel was deeply broken on the inside but well put together on the outside. Chanel would second guess herself a lot; she struggled with assertiveness, self-esteem, confidence, and value. She didn't see herself as valuable. Chanel would regularly down herself and all the things she ever did wrong in life. She didn't know how to be grateful to herself. She didn't know how to show herself mercy. She would instead condemn herself for everything she did wrong.

Finally, her relationship with God was too broken. She knew God existed, and she knew that he loved her. But she didn't always believe it. Chanel wasn't convinced. *How can God love someone like me? I mean, look at me?* She then started to replay all the times she did wrong in her life. *Guilty, guilty, guilty.* Her voice would say in her head, and Chanel believed it.

She recalled her sexual past before the rape. All the boys she had done stuff with. She remembered when she let the boy finger her on the back of the bus in middle school, she remembered how confused she was about her sexuality and the amounts of lesbian porn she watched or just porn in general, she remembered the boy who broke her heart and how she tried to sabotage his relationship to his new woman, and she remembered everything.

She then started to remember the rape. How it happened, where it happened, how she responded, how he responded, her life afterward, and the pain she felt. Chanel was so enthralled in her thoughts; she forgot she was driving.

"Honk…honk…"

"What?" Chanel said as she looked out her driver's window.

"Move," the passenger in the car next to her said. Chanel didn't realize she was sitting at a green light. Oh, I must have zoned out. She thought to herself.

"Sorry," she mouthed as she pushed the gas. Chanel looked down at the time; it was only 11:30 a.m. Her next class wasn't until 3:30 pm that day. She still had enough time to take a nap before heading to the library and then lesson afterward. Chanel pulled up in front of her condo, and saw her neighbor sitting on his balcony. *That man is fine,* she said to herself. Chanel gathered her things and exited her car. As she walked up to the building her neighbor looked down from his balcony and said,

"Greetings, young lady."

"Hello," she responded.

"Oh, you're speaking to me?" he asked.

"Uhm, what is that supposed to me?"

"Well, normally you look at me all funny and roll your eyes. I'm shocked you said something this time". Chanel rolled her eyes at him.

"I don't owe you nothing," she responded.

"No, you don't. But it wouldn't kill you to smile, will it? Sometimes you come off as unapproachable. You're a beautiful girl, but have a horrible attitude." He said to with a stern gaze. Chanel studied his face. She couldn't respond. Instead, she ignored his comment and walked right into the building without giving it a second thought. She let herself into her apartment and flung herself onto her bed. She heard a small knock at the door. Slightly alarmed, Chanel approached the door cautiously. No one knows she lives there besides her aunt. As she looked through the peephole, she saw it was her neighbor. Chanel instantly became annoyed. She slightly cracked the door, "How may I help you?" she asked in a severe tone.

"I wanted to apologize for how I came at you back there."

"Oh, okay. Is that all?"

"Yep," he answered.

"Thanks for the apology. Have a nice day," she said as she closed her door. She went back into her room and laid in her bed. Another knock at the door. Chanel trying to reserve her anger, gracefully got out of her bed and opened the door.

"Yes?" she asked

"Did I offend you?"

"What makes you ask that?"

"Well, you closed the door as if I bothered you," he replied. Chanel became irritated by her neighbor. She didn't understand why he was forcing himself on her.

"I'm sorry. I'm just a little tired, and I need a nap because I have a lot to accomplish today," Chanel replied.

"Aw ok."

"Is there anything else you need?"

"Nah, that's all."

"Ok, great. Goodbye," Chanel responded sarcastically with a fake smile as she closed the door. She turned and walked back to her bedroom. She laid down, set her alarm clock, and got herself situated. She closed her eyes, hoping to fall asleep. She tossed, and turned, tossed and turned and nothing happened. Ugh! She looked over at her clock as it read 12:00 pm. *Okay, don't panic; you still have plenty of enough time for sleep.* So she tried again. She closed her eyes and tried to relax as much as possible. But still, no luck. *Ugh! Why can't I fall asleep!* Chanel laid in her bed, she glanced up at the ceiling and started counting the lines left behind from the paintbrush. Slowly her thought began to drift to her neighbor. She laid there thinking about her interaction with him, and suddenly she found herself getting wet at the thought of him. *NO!* She suddenly sat straight up in her bed. She couldn't believe that she found herself attracted to that man! It was improper! It was unlike her! She barely knew him, and they hardly get along with each other. She shook her head at the thought and laid back down. She looked over at her clock and saw that it read 12:30 pm. *Okay, I still have some time to catch a little shut-eye.* Chanel laid there, and closed her eyes and finally drifted to sleep.

With a sudden bolt of energy, Chanel shot up from her sleep! *What time is it?* She saw that it was dark outside. She looked over at her clock, and it read 5:00 pm. *Omg, are you serious! I slept through my alarm and missed class. Oh well, there's nothing I can do about it now.* She rose from her bed and made her way to the bathroom. She sat on the toilet and mentally ran through her schedule list of activities for the day. Since she missed class and it was getting dark outside, she opted to stay in and work on her class assignments instead. She typically likes working in the library, but today she didn't feel like it. *Oh, my computer is still in the car.* So she got up, flushed the toilet, washed her hands, and made her way outside to retrieve her computer. Once outside, Chanel saw that her neighbor was still out there.

"I thought you had a busy schedule for today," he said to her backside. Chanel turned and looked at him, made a face and walked to her car. She grabbed her computer, and chirped the lock. As she walked back into the building, her neighbor called to her from his balcony,

"Excuse me," he spoke.

"Yes," she replied.

"Uhm, are you sure I don't offend you?"

"I'm positive."

"Well, why you act all stank whenever I speak to you?"

"What is to you that I act stank?"

"Well maybe I want to be your friend?" Chanel stood in shock. "Oh, you wanna be my friend?" that came as a surprise to her. Feeling guilty, Chanel responded.

"I'm sorry. I didn't realize you wanted to be my friend."

"Well, yea, I would like to be, but you're very mean and unapproachable."

"When you say unapproachable, what do you mean by that?"

"It means that you're not easy to talk to, and it's not easy to start a conversation with you. You don't look friendly to approach, and it makes it difficult to engage." Chanel began to feel bad. Well, it wouldn't hurt to have a little friendship with him. What's the worst that can happen?

"Okay, I'm willing to be your friend." They both shared a smile. *That man is fine!* Chanel thought to herself.

"well, I don't want to keep you. I'll let you go."

"Okay, goodnight."

"Goodnight." They both closed their doors, and Chanel took a long sigh. She was ashamed of her behavior. But at least he was understanding and just wanted a friendship. He seems like a good person. Chanel didn't sense any bad feelings from him. She let the idea of starting a friendship roll over in her mind, and she smiled at the thought of it. Let's see how this goes. But, now let's get to work. She sat down on her bed and got to work. She emailed her professor and apologized for missing class she reviewed her chem work, research studies work, and filled several orders from her website. When she checked back with the time it was 9:45 pm.

"Whew, I got a lot a lot of work done,…" Chanel patted herself on the back. She was super happy to have accomplished getting so much finished. She was ready for a long hot bubble bath. Chanel walked into her kitchen and heard her neighbor coming down the stairs. *"I wonder what he's doing,"* she thought to herself. She peeped through the peephole and saw him heading out the door. He appeared to be talking on the phone. Chanel just looked him over. He was indeed okay. She marveled over his build, muscular arms, mustache, braids, and light skin. She found herself getting wet thinking about him.

"No," she scoffed at herself, *"I will not go there. He is only my neighbor."* She backed away from the door and made her way into the kitchen. She reached and grabbed herself a cup from the cupboard and poured herself a nice tall glass of water. She savored the taste of the water. It was cold and refreshing. She began to daydream about her neighbor. She imagined what his hands would feel like on her body. How his body felt against hers, how his tongue felt between.

"Knock knock." Caught completely off guard, she almost dropped her cup.

"Yes," she answered back as she tried to get herself together.

"It's me," the voice replied.

"Me who?"

"Your neighbor."

"Okay, one second," she replied. *I wonder what he could want at this time of night.*

Chanel opened her door and answered "yes." with hesitation. Picking up on her nervousness, he responded, "I'm sorry, I didn't mean to startle you."

"It's okay. Did you need something?"

"Yea, I wanted to know if you were free so we can talk?"

"About?"

"Anything honestly, it doesn't matter." Chanel was taken off guard. *I knew he said he wanted a friendship, but this was a little too fast for her liking.* Trying to play it cool, Chanel responded back.

"Okay, well, how was your day?"

"My day was good. And you don't have to all formal like, how was your day. That's real cute."

"I mean, what else you want me to say," Chanel chuckled. *This man is nuts.*

"Shoot idk, ask me if I got my thumb cut off today." They both laughed in unison. Chanel made her way to the steps and took a seat. He followed suit and sat on the cold floor.

"You know, I thought you were stunning when I first saw you."

"Really," Chanel replied.

"Yes. I thought you were very attractive."

"Aww, that's sweet, thanks."

"It's good, no biggie."

"Okay, cool, so how old are you?" Chanel asked.

"35, you?"

"19"

"Oh, you're a baby."

'No, I'm not."

"Yea, you are, no wonder why you act like that," he responded. Chanel rolled her eyes at his comment.

'I want you to know that I'm very mature for my age, thank you very much."

'Oh, is that right?"

'Yes, I'm 19, but I have my condo, a business, and I'm a senior in college studying biochemistry."

"For real?"

"Yes."

"I'm impressed he responded. Well excuse me," he said with a smirk. "Brains and beauty. How about that." Chanel felt herself getting red at his compliment.

'What about you, what do you do?"

"Oh, I work at a factory; I help build airplane parts."

"Oh, I bet that's exciting."

"It is. I love my job. I like working with my hands. I like to create things." He said. I bet you do, Chanel thought to herself. She found herself fantasizing about him and his hands on her body. *Stop it!*

"Yea, when I'm not working, I'm traveling."

'Oh, I would love to travel."

"Really?"

"Yes, I would love to see the world."

"Well, maybe you can?"

"How so?" Chanel questioned.

"You can come with me," he said with a grin. Chanel felt her vagina get hot through the fabric. Trying to play it cool, she replied, "I bet you would love that."

'I would. I get lonely sometimes, and having someone there with me along for the ride would be amazing," he continued. Chanel smiled at the thought. 'I'll think about it," she said jokingly. They both laughed in unison. The two continued talking in the stairwell for hours. Chanel forgot all about her bubble bath. Chanel looked down at her watch and noticed it was 11:15 pm.

"Oh, I need to get back in so I can get some rest for tomorrow."

"Oh yea, I understand." Chanel got up and brushed herself off. She saw caught him watching her. Feeling his eyes over her she quickly finished and walked over to her door.

"Goodnight sir."

"Sir? you don't have to be that formal with me."

"Okay."

"You can call me Trey."

"okay, goodnight Trey," Chanel walked into her apartment and closed the door behind her. *She leans back against the door and took a deep sigh. I must be careful around him.* She let her mind linger at the thought of him for a few more minutes before walking into the bathroom and running her bathwater. She poured lavender scented bubble bath and eucalyptus bath salt into the water for much-needed relaxation. She undressed and slid into her steaming hot bubble bath. She laid back into the tub and savored how the water covered her body.

"This was so much needed." She couldn't remember the last time she unwinds. She's been so busy lately that it was hard to schedule some me-time for her. She continues to lay in the bathwater and soaked. She laid there for so long that she began to drift off to sleep. *That means it's time to get*

out. She hurried and washed her body and quickly got out. She dried off and oiled herself with coconut oil because she read somewhere that it's good for the skin. Afterward, she slipped into her silk Victoria secret pj's. As she made her way to the bed, she dumped her dirty clothes in the basket, and laid down in the bed. Before she could even fully close her eyes, she was sound asleep.

The next morning she awakens earlier than usual. She looked over at her alarm clock, and the time read 6:30 am. She rolled her eyes, and turned back over, and tried to get more sleep. Another few minutes go by and she moves around to look at her alarm clock. The time read 7:15. *Okay, I guess it's time to get up*. She gently picked herself up out of bed and removed the crust from her eye. She sat on the edge of her bed still, half asleep. Then she heard someone walking down the steps. The walls of this place are thin. She wondered who could be up at that time in the morning. She quickly got up and walked towards the living room window. She peered through the blinds, saw her neighbor with his workout gear again and got into his car. After several minutes of sitting there, he finally pulled off. *He must workout at the gym. That must be how he stays in shape*. Backing away from the window still, in la-la land she almost tripped over a box.

"Ouch," she said as she rubbed her stubbed toe. She still had lots of unpacking to do. *Well, let's get to it*. So, she made herself a cup of coffee, and started to unpack her boxes in the living room. She unpacked every box, and broke it down by 9. That's when she heard her neighbor return. She hurried to the door and opened it to meet him in the hallway.

"Did you have a nice workout this morning?" she spoke as she sipped her cup of coffee. Her neighbor turned around and said,

"Well, good morning to you too," as he looked her over. Chanel forgot she still had on her pj's with silk shorts and cami top. "Look like you just woke up out of bed," he continued.

"Oh no, I've been up since 7:15 this morning."

"Oh yea."

"Mhm."

"Well let me get freshened up and I'll knock on your door when I'm done."

"Sure." Both of them reentered their apartments. *Maybe I should put on some clothes too.* So she hastily put her clothes on and sat on her bed. *Why am I so excited to see this man?* She brushed off her excitement. She didn't want to seem like she some kid in the candy store. To busy herself, she started to unpack more boxes. Just as she was making her way into the hallway, she heard a faint knock at the door.

"Yes," she answered as she opened the door. She was dressed in Nike joggers and a fitted t-shirt.

"I see you changed clothes."

"Yes, had to come out of those pj's. I see you are refreshed and clean."

"I am," as he looked her over again.

"I always catch you staring at me."

"You do the same to me." Chanel felt her face become hot.

"Aww, you're blushing," replied with a smirk. Chanel continued to blush but felt herself become alive down below.

"You gotta man?" he asked.
"No, why?"
"Just curious. So what do you do for a living?"
"No, tell me?" Chanel said. She wanted to know.
'Well."
"Well, what?"
"Well, I was wondering"
"Wondering about?"
"Wondering if you would let me be that for you?"

The Unknown

Chanel was at her daytime job day-dreaming about her new neighbor. *I wonder what his day is like?* Chanel couldn't focus on her work, that she didn't see her coworker approach her.

"Girl, what you over there thinking about?" her coworker asked.

"Oh nothing."

"You lying. You are smiling and looking all up in the ceiling. What man got you smiling like that?"

"lol, it's nothing Bebe." Chanel responded. Bebe, an older black woman, old enough to be Chanel's momma rolled her eyes at Chanel.

"Girl, please, I know that look when I see it. You are thinking about a man. But that's okay you don't have to tell me." Bebe said as she took a seat at her desk across from Chanel. Chanel and Bebe were good friends. Chanel confined to Bebe about everything. Her rape, her low self-esteem, her suicidal thoughts, her suicidal attempt, everything. Bebe to Chanel was a motherly figure. Chanel couldn't be this intimate with her mother, and she was afraid to share this with her aunt. But with Bebe, she felt safe. She felt heard. She didn't feel judged. The two had a fantastic friendship. Chanel knew that Bebe would call her out on her crap and not hold it against her.

"So tell me about your new place?" Bebe asked Chanel.

"Girl, it is so bombed. I love it. It's a one-bedroom condo, with vaulted ceilings, spacious rooms, a patio, carpet in the bedroom, hardwood floors throughout the house, it's just marvelous!"

"Oh, that sounds nice."

"How much you paying a month?"

"$650."

"Oh, Not bad!"

"Can you afford it?"

"Yes, with this job and my hair selling business on the side, I make triple the amount. So I'm good. Plus, I have my refund check coming from school. So I will be set!"

"Okay! I heard that!"

"You see any fine men over there?" Bebe asked. Chanel hesitated. She didn't want to tell Bebe about her neighbor off-right. So, instead, she decided to play it cool.

"I've seen a few guys. I wasn't looking at them like that, though. Girl, I don't want no drama."

'Girl, I feel you. You don't want any drama where you lay yo head at. You never know these men to be crazy these days. You heard that story about that young lady who got killed by this guy she turned down?"

"Nah! What happened?"

"Girl, one of these young guys tried to talk to a girl, and she rejected him. So he killed her."

"Omg! Are you serious? I hate when guys do that. Masculinity is so fragile that they can't take rejection. It's sickening!"

"Very!"

"Yea, you be careful. Don't be inviting crazy men over to your house. You never know what they will do to you." Bebe said. Chanel instantly had a flashback to her rape. She remembered she invited the guy over to her dorm room. It was day-time hours. They went to a day party, and he had a few drinks. He was older than Chanel. She remembers they came back to her dorm room to make-out and close burn.

"Chanel. Are you okay?" Bebe asked. She noticed Chanel became silent during the conversation.

"Yes, I'm fine." she responded.

"Okay," Bebe started, "It's okay to date guys Chanel. Don't be afraid to get back out there. And if you need anything, just call me!" Bebe said as she came over and rubbed Chanel's hand.

"Thanks, Bebe" Chanel responded.

"Whew, girl, what time is it?"

"It's getting close to the time you clock out?" Bebe said. Chanel looked down at her watch. It read at 2:55 pm. She can clock out at 3:00 pm.

"Oh, let me start breaking down and packing up." Chanel said out loud. She logged out of her computer, cleaned her desk space, grabbed her purse, used the restroom, retrieved her lunch from the employee refrigerator, and made her way to the time clock. The time clock read 3:03. *Perfect*, she said.

As she made her way to the elevator, Bebe stood in the doorway.

"So what you got planned today?"

"Idk," Chanel said, "I might go to the library and do some studying. I need to refresh myself on my bio work. Don't want to fall behind."

"Aw, okay. That's good. I'm glad you about your schooling. Just don't forget to have fun."

"Of course." Chanel responded. Just then, her elevator arrived. She stepped on and pressed button 2A.

"And don't forget to go out on a date! You're a pretty girl. Make some friends. Stop being so secluded!" Bebe yelled out as the elevator doors closed.

"I will." Chanel yelled back. *I hope she heard me.* Chanel found herself day-dreaming about her neighbor again. *I might stop home and see what he's up to.* The elevator let her off at her floor, and Chanel walked to her car. She chirped the lock, got in, set her purse and lunch in the passenger seat, and started the car. She adjusted her mirrors and pulled out the lot. On the way home, she just kept thinking about her neighbor. *Chanel girl, you are silly; that is a grown man. You don't want to get involved with him.* She was in a light. She contemplated if she was making the right decision going home to meet to see if her neighbor is there. *Maybe just a quick pop in and back out the door. I don't want to seem desperate.* She continued her drive home until she finally made it. Chanel parked her car in her spot and grabbed all her stuff. She looked to the second-floor balcony window and to see if he was home. He wasn't standing outside so, she wasn't sure. Well, since I'm here, I can at least drop my lunch off. So she entered the apartment building and walked to her door. Chanel was opening her door when she heard the main building door open. Chanel looked, and it was her neighbor.

"Hey." she said as she opened her door.

"Hey." he responded.

"What's up?" she said.

'Oh nothing, just getting in. I went and cut my sister's grass."

"Aw, okay?"

"You, just getting in from work?"

"From selling weave?"

"Nah, I have another job."

"Aw, so you have two jobs?"

"Yes."

'Aw, okay. What do you do at this job?"

"I work at a call center where I talk to patients about prescriptions and stuff."

"Aw okay. I was wondering because you told me you sell weave."

"Yea"

"I was just curious how you pay your bills selling weave?"

"Lol yes, I make a lot of money doing it."

"Oh word?"

"Yes, I'm rich.. lol" they laughed in unison.

"And you go to school?"

"Yep!"

"Aw, okay, what do you go to school for?"

"I'm a science degree. Biochemistry to be exact."

"Oh, that's what's up. So you smart, beautiful, got a place of your own and single." he replied as he licked his lips at her. Catching him, flicking his tongue in her direction, Chanel became instantly aroused.

"yep," as she tried to gain her composure.

"Have you ever been intimate with a man before?" he questioned. Chanel felt a bit uneasy with him asking her that type of question. So instead of her answering right out, she instead answered his question with a question.

"What makes you ask me that?" she responded.

"Just curious." he answered.

"I don't think that's any of your business." Chanel responded. Any sexual excitement she initially felt was now gone, thanks to him.

"Uhm, I have to get ready to head out to the library. Caught you around, Trey". Noticing how uncomfortable she became, he quickly apologized.

"I'm sorry, I didn't mean to make you feel uncomfortable."

"Oh, it no big deal," she lied. It was indeed a huge deal to her. And she felt violated that he would even consider asking her that question. So she bided him a farewell and entered her apartment highly disturbed. She entered her kitchen and poured herself a cup of coffee. *Dang, the conversation was going smooth, then splat! He ruined it!* She tried her hardest to forget the conversation she just had in the hallway. Then she heard a knock at her door. She approached her door and looked through the peephole. It was him again. She scoffed. *What does he want?*

Chanel brushed the hair out of her eyes and smoothed her shirt. She tried her best to present herself calm.

"Yes?", as she opened the door.

"Hey, I just wanted to say sorry again. I didn't mean to make you feel uncomfortable. I always want you to feel comfortable."

"I completely understand. No hard feelings, honest."

"Are you sure?"

"Positive."

"Okay."

"Alright, have a nice day." Chanel responded. She softly shut the door behind her. She lingered around the door a few minutes longer just in case he decided to knock on the door again. She walked into the bathroom to wash the coffee taste out of her mouth, and only then, another knock at her door. *OMG*. Chanel was becoming annoyed with him continually knocking on her door. *What the hell does he want!* She ignored him. She continued to rinse her mouth, and again another knock at the door.

"hold on, please!" Chanel called out! *My lord, what does this man want. I've already told him I'm not angry and no hard feelings; why bother?* As she dried her mouth with a paper towel she came around the corner to answer the door.

"Yes?"

"Hey, I was making a crab boil today and wanted to know if you wanted some? Chanel made a face. *Is he offering me food?*

"Uh, sure?' she responded.

"Why the face?"

"I thought it was weird, nothing personal."

"What you mean weird? What's weird about that?"

"Nothing, I've never had neighbors offer me food before."

"Oh, well, I'm different. Trust me."

"Okay, I trust you, and sure I don't mind a crab boil. Are you from down south?"

"Yes, actually, born and raised?"

"Oh, really. What state? And, how did you get up here to Philly?"

"I was born in Texas. I moved to Philly right after I graduated from college. I went to school up here."

"Oh, wow. That's dope. Do you miss your family at all?"

"Sometimes. I visit my momma every summer, though."

"Aw, I bet she's always happy to see you."

"Of course. So how much you want?"

"Whatever I can have, I love seafood."

"Me too!"

"Yea, it's nice to meet other seafood lovers."

"I know, a lot of people don't like the smell. How do you cook your fish?"

"It depends on what I'm in the mood for. Boiled, sautéed, baked, fried, on ice, it doesn't matter. What kind of seasoning do you put on yours?"

"The typical. Lemon, butter, garlic, old bay, salt, pepper, some parsley."

"Oh, that sounds good." Chanel responded. She started to remember his question from earlier that day.

"Hey, what made you ask if I've ever been with a man before?"

"Well, I was just curious, honestly?"

"Why were you curious?"

"I was just trying to get to know you, that's all."

"Oh, I guess."

"Did it make you feel uncomfortable?"

"Yes, because I found it inappropriate."

"Oh, I'm sorry. I didn't mean to offend you. My apologies."

"Yea, thanks!" Chanel thought about it for a second, "I wanted to apologize to you too about earlier. I didn't mean to come off like that. I probably could have said it differently. I just don't talk about my intimate life."

"Oh, I understand. I'm sorry I made you feel uncomfortable." he responded. Chanel just looked down. *Maybe he didn't mean any harm. Perhaps he was just trying to get to know me.* There was an awkward silence between the two of them. Chanel looked up and saw him looking at her again with his bedroom eyes.

"Hey, how about you come over to my place for lunch?" Chanel was taken back. She barely knew this man, but she was very intrigued by him and seemed okay. I mean, what's the worst that could happen?

"Uhm, sure."

"Are you sure?" he asked.

"Yes. Are we going to be doing anything else?"

"I mean, we can watch what's on tv. It's not like a date or anything like that."

"Okay, cool, that doesn't sound too bad."

"What time you want me to come over?"

"About 5 pm."

"Alright, see you at five." Chanel responded. She walked back into her condo and closed the door behind her. She was excited. She ran into her room to text her friend Courtney,

"Hey girl."

"Hey."

"What you doing?"

"Nothing, you."

"Oh nothing, but tell me why my neighbor invited me over to his place at five."

"Really? How old is he?"

"He's way older than me?"

"Girl, like how old?"

"35"

"Oh lord Chanel."

"What?"

"Be careful girl; you don't know what that man has up his sleeve!"

"You're right, but he seems so nice."

"I'll give it a chance and see what he's talking about."

"Alright girl, be safe."

"I will." Chanel responded. She laid out on her bed wondering, what all they would do over at his house. She looked down at her watch; the time read 4:15 pm. She figured she had enough time to unpack her bedroom and take a small shower before heading over to Trey's.

At 5:00 pm Chanel knocked on Trey's door. "Hold on," he called out. She waited patiently. Then she heard the lock turn and the door open.

"Welcome." he said with a smile.

"Hello." Chanel smiled back and walked into his condo. She could tell he cleaned up. He had posters of famous NBA players on his wall, a signed jersey, some of his trophies sat near an end table. Near his windows, he had flower pots with some cactus growing, a nice sized deep chocolate sectional that set against his wall, across from his sectional was a gigantic 65-inch flatscreen TV. In the middle of the floor, sat a leather rectangle tabletop. On top of the table laid some open mail and a small pint of alcohol. His wall above the sectional held black urban art. The colors filled the room. His space felt very comfortable with her. She liked it. His bedroom door was closed.

"Have a seat." he said as he ushered her to a seat on his oversized sectional.

"Sure." Chanel said as she made her way over. He walked into the kitchen and came back out with a plate full of crab legs, crawfish, boiled eggs, sausage, corn, potatoes, and shrimp.

"Thank you." Chanel gleamed. It looked like a lot of food. She was excited.

"No problem." he replied, as he took a seat next to her.

"You're condo is nice."

"Thanks, I need to clean it." he replied. They both laughed together. Chanel felt herself getting comfortable and sat back further on the sectional.

"Would you like something to drink?"

"Yes, you got some water."

"Yep." He got up and went into the kitchen and brought Chanel back some water. Chanel took her first bite of shrimp, and it tastes so good. The juice started to drip off her lips.

"You need a napkin?" he laughed.

"Lol, yes! It's so good."

"Alright, I'll bring you some." He exited out of the living room again and retrieved some napkins from the kitchen.

"Thank you so much. You are so nice."

"No problem at all." he responded. Chanel noticed that he didn't have any food.

"Are you going to eat?"

"Nah, I was eating them as they were coming out of the pot into the pan." He laughed.

"Oh." Chanel smiled back.

"Yea, I couldn't help myself."

Chanel sat quietly, listening to his laughter, fill the room. He seemed so at ease and relaxed. He felt extremely comfortable. She wanted to know more about him. Bringing her out of her thoughts, he said, "So, can I ask you a question?"

"Sure."

"Are you dating anyone?"

"No." she answered.

"Are you interested in dating?"

"Yes."

"Why haven't you?"

"I haven't found someone that I can see myself with?"

"Oh, how old are you again, if you don't mind me asking?"

"I'm 19."

"Oh, you're young." He replied

"I'm not too young." Chanel replied. She wanted to prove that just because she's 19, doesn't mean anything.

"I'm 35."

"I remember you telling me."

"Yea, I did tell you this before." he commented as he reached for the pint of alcohol on his leather rectangle round table.

"Oh, you're like 16 years older than me."

"Yea, 16 years more experience." he said as he made eye contact with her and grinned. Chanel, felt his laughter in the base of her belly. It made it's way down to her most intimate parts and begun to arouse her.

"So, are you dating anyone?" she asked

"Nah, I'm single. I've been single for years." he said. That comment rubbed Chanel the wrong way. She wasn't sure why, but it did. She wanted to probe more.

"Why come?"

"My last relationship didn't work out." Chanel still wasn't satisfied with his answer. But she knew not to probe too deep.

"Oh, I'm sorry to hear that."

"Yea, I walked in on her cheating on me?"

"Really?" Chanel was stunned. *Well, that was easy.*

"Yes. I came in and caught her having sex in our bed. I tried to fight ole dude, and she was screaming. I mean, all the neighbors knew. Somebody called the police. It was terrible. I was deeply hurt. She and I had been together since high school. We went to different colleges and stuff, but we tried to make it work. I caught her over the summer break. She had an apartment in our hometown because she went to college there. She had a full ride to the university. I was in Philly. They let us out early for summer break. So I was planning to surprise her. So I pulled up to her crib and walked in."

"Wow, I'm sorry you had to experience that."

"Yea! It hurt me so much when I saw that."

"That must have been pretty rough for you."

"yea, I've been single since."

"I bet. I can understand your pain."

"Yea..." he spoke quietly. Chanel felt terrible for the man. He was so fine, and she wondered why someone would mistreat him.

"Well, you're not the only one who's been hurt before," Chanel spoke softly.

"I, too, have experienced hurt and trauma."

"Really? But you're so young. What possibly could you have experience?"

"I got my heartbroken by this guy I loved too. We were high school sweethearts. He was so sweet to me. We did everything with each other. You know typical love bird stuff."

"Yea. So what happened?"

"Well, we had a minor break up, at first. Like you, we were dating long distance too. It was hard trying to maintain a relationship. So he broke up with me. I was crushed. I would try to get back with him, and he would always deny me and say that he wasn't ready for a relationship. He wanted to explore college. That so hurt me. Now mind you, our colleges weren't that far from each other. Yes, we were in different states, but the distance was drivable in my mind anyway. Like an hour drive between us. So anyway, my friends at the time told us about a party at the school he was going to. I said yes, hoping that I would see him at the party and maybe we could talk about it. So you know, I get all dressed up. We drive up there and see him at the party, all hugged up on some chick. I go over there and snatch him off the girl. Like is this what we are doing now? He got all defensive and was like, what are you doing here. We started arguing in the middle of the party. The girl then interjects herself and says he's her man now. He doesn't want me anymore. I'm broke and busted- all types of stuff. So I tell the girl to back off and leave me alone. But she wouldn't listen. So then I think I pushed the girl because she was getting all in my face. Then the girl pushed me back and called me a b****, and boom, we were fighting at the party. Somebody called the police. My friends had to drag me off the school property. So we drive back thinking we were in the clear. But nah, my ex-bf told them my name and what school I went to, so the police came there and it was this huge ordeal. Long story short, he broke my heart. I was crushed."

"I'm sorry that happened to you," he started. Chanel looked up to meet his gaze. His words seemed so sincere, and his eye was apologetic.

"Yea, I have plenty more stories, but I don't want to tell you all my stories just yet."

"Why is that?"

"Well, I just want to leave some mystery."

"Oh, is that what you call it?" he as chuckled. "Let's change the subject," he replied. He got up and went into the kitchen. Chanel smoothed her outfit out. She pulled out her cell phone and used the glass as a mirror to fix her hair. Trey appeared in the archway and said,

"Would you like a drink? I know you asked for water, but I also have wine or beer."

"Lol, no thanks. But thank you," she replied. Trey came back and sat on the couch next to Chanel.

"You know you are wonderful. And you deserved to be treated with respect. And it hurts me that someone would do that to you. You don't deserve that type of treatment. If you were mine, I would worship the ground you walk on. A woman like you should be treated like a Queen." Trey said as he took a sip of his beer. He sat back in disbelief. Chanel watched him. *If I was his? Wow.*

"Yea, I would be wonderful to you. I would show you off and everything. It just hurts me to know that someone you loved could turn out to be so cold. He's trash for that."

"Aww, thank you, I'm flattered you find yourself attracted to me, honestly."

"What you mean?" Trey looked Chanel in her eyes. "You are beautiful. I mean, besides the age difference, you are everything that a man would want in his women. Smart, educated, independent, honest, goal-oriented, kept, sexy" as he dropped his eyes and began biting and licking his lips. Chanel eyes grew wide and she sat back at his gestures.

"I'm sorry. I don't mean to be too straight-forward."

"It's okay," Chanel lied. She felt a little squeamish at the same time turned on. "I think it's best if I get going." Chanel immediately saw the disappointment on his face. They both stood up and walked to the door. "Okay," he replied, really sour. Chanel caught it. She felt bad. But she knew it was best. So she reached out to open the door. Trey seeing this, said, "Allow me," and reached to open the door instead. Their hands touched. Trey looked Chanel in the eyes and smiled while she blushed.

"Thanks, Trey, I had a fun time being here with you. And thanks for the free food. I enjoyed it. You're a great cook." she said. She wanted to cheer him up about her leaving.

"Thank you for letting me be of service to you. We should do this again."

"Of course," Chanel replied. She liked the sound of that. Trey opened his door and stepped out of the way so that she may leave. Chanel smiled as she stepped into the hallway. She turned back around and found him staring at her.

"Lol, you just let it be known that you like me, huh?" Chanel said jokingly.

Trey smiled, "I'm a man; that's what I'm supposed to do" they both laughed in unison as Chanel walked down the steps.

"Thanks again, Trey."

"No problem… oh, what you're name?"

"Chanel."

"I hope to see you again, Ms. Chanel," he cooed. Chanel smiled one last time and walked down the steps to her condo. Once inside, she leaned back against the door. *Wow, this man is something. He's so attentive, charming, sexy, and caring.* Chanel let the thought of him linger in her mind. It tickled her to know that this man was so interested in her. He cared about her feelings and well-being. In that short moment, his attentiveness and affirmation words were more than what she received from her father. She was so excited. She ran into her bedroom, and got on her phone and texted her friend Courtney about her encounter with Trey.

"Hey, girl, I'm back from Trey's place."

"Oh, that's his name. You all on first name bases now?"

"Yea," Chanel said, smiling, "He is so nice. He cooked a seafood boil and shared it with me. We talked. We're getting to know each other. He told me how beautiful I was and how he would love to date a woman like me…"

"So how old is he again?"

"Uhm, 35."

"He's 35, Chanel. I think that might be a little too old for you. You're only 19. Yea, you're brilliant and graduated high school early, but I just don't know about this."

"I know…"

"Chanel, I don't like this. You are talking to this older man. You don't know anything about you, really. You are still learning yourself. You're prey to him. Older men prey on younger women all the time," Courtney replied. That pissed Chanel off.

"You know nothing about him. You're judging him. He's nice. I would know if someone is trying to run game on me, and I don't sense that in him."

"Whatever, girl. Please be careful Chanel."

"I will. Promise."

Chanel couldn't believe that Courtney was acting this way. She had no idea how kind, caring, and attentive Trey was. He was a nice guy. Just then, Chanel heard a knock at her front door.

"Hold on, please." she called out. She wondered who that could be. She looked through the peephole, and it was her Aunt. Excitement washed over her body.

"Hey, Auntie!" Chanel exclaimed as she opened the door.

"Hey, baby… how are you?" they embraced each other. Chanel adored her Aunt. She was the only solid mother figure Chanel has ever known.

"C'mon in," Chanel motioned as she ushered her Aunt inside. "So this is it!" Chanel beamed as she threw her hands in the air. Her Aunt surveyed the condo.

"This is a wonderful, Chanel; I mean wonderful. I am so proud of you!"

"Let me give you a tour," Chanel replied as she grabbed her Aunt by the hand. She first took her into the living room, then the kitchen, the bathroom, her bedroom, and a small balcony off the kitchen!

"Isn't it beautiful?"

"yes, it is, baby! This place is nice just for you!"

"Thanks, Auntie. Thank you for being there for me. Helping me stay focused."

"Oh baby, you know I love you and only want the best for you" they embraced each other again.

"Okay, so I bought you over some greens, mac n cheese, sweet potatoes, and honey ham."

"Omg, yes!!" Chanel exclaimed, "I've needed a home-cooked meal."

"I bet you have, baby! I'm already knowing. I know what it's like to be on your own. When I first started on my own, your uncle and I had nothing. We figured it out along the way," her Aunt continued. She loved hearing the stories of her Aunt and Uncle how they lived before he died of a heart attack at the tender age of 39. Before her Aunt could continue, there was another knock at the door. Her Aunt was startled.

"Visitors already?" her Aunt asked. Chanel felt embarrassed. She knew who it was knocking at the door.

"Hold on for a second," she said as she walked to the door and opened it. It was Trey.

"Hey, can I talk to you later? My Aunt is here."

"Oh, my bad." he said. "Yea, just knock on the door later." he called out as he walked back up the steps. Chanel closed the door and turned to see her aunt's brow furrowed.

"Who is that?" she asked.

"Oh, it's no one. That's just my neighbor."

"You're neighbor." Her aunt said with a small puzzlement.

"Yes, ma'am, my neighbor. I'm trying to meet all my neighbors and see what they are like," Chanel lied. She wanted more than that with him.

"Aw, okay." her Aunt said with hesitation.

"Don't worry Auntie, everything will be fine."

"Okay," her Aunt replied. Chanel knew her Aunt would disapprove of her befriending a man ten years her age. Sensing her Aunt dissatisfaction, Chanel changed the subject.

"Would you like to help me finish unpacking? I'm pretty much done in the living room. I still have my bedroom and some parts of the kitchen."

"Sure, baby, You didn't think I just came over here to feed you and not help you unpack?"

"I can always count on you Auntie." Chanel walked back into the living room and embraced her Aunt. She was indeed the best thing that Chanel could ever hope for! She was beyond grateful to have her in her life.

"Alright baby, let's get started." her Aunt replied.

The two women worked tirelessly. Each one packing boxes, unpacking them, and breaking the boxes down afterwards. By the time they finished packing, the sun was beginning to set. Chanel stood in the hallway and viewed the condo with fresh eyes. She felt overcome with joy.

"Wow, I can officially say I'm home," Chanel squealed.

"Yes, you are, baby! You are officially home. And Chanel, I couldn't be any prouder." her Aunt chimed.

"Well, I have you to thank. If it wasn't for you, Idk where I would be." Chanel replied. "Well, are you hungry? Would you like to stay and eat with me? I know you packed those plates sky high. I will have enough food for days!" They both laughed

"You know Auntie gotta take care of her baby." She replied as she gently pinched Chanel's cheek.

"Unfortunately, Auntie gotta go! My show is coming on, and I don't want to miss it! But maybe next Sunday you come over, and we have ourselves a Sunday dinner."

"Oh, that sounds amazing. You can count me in." Chanel replied. Her Aunt made her way to the door before abruptly stopping in front of it.

"Chanel," she called out. Sensing that something was troubling her aunt, she quickly ran to be by her side. "Yes, ma'am." she answered.

"That man, how long have you been communicating with him?"

"Not long, only a few days?"

"Uh, be careful, honey."

"What makes you say that?" Chanel asked.

"I'm not sure. It's just something about him." her Aunt continued, "Something just seems off." she said.

"He seems like such a nice guy," Chanel replied, confused.

"They always do in the beginning. I just want you to be safe." Chanel felt uneasy at her aunt's warning. She didn't understand why she would say such a thing. She just doesn't know Trey, that's all. Instead of pressing the issue any further, she simply said,

"Yes, ma'am." Chanel opened the door for her aunt and walked her out to her car. Chanel stood on the curb and waved goodbye to her aunt as she pulled off. She returned to her condo, still replaying her aunt words in her head. *What she means by "he seems off?" How could he be off? For the most part, all they do is talk. He apologies whenever he makes a mistake, or say and do anything that makes me feel uncomfortable. He's ultra-sweet. He's charming. He's reticent and to himself.* Besides that incident that happened when she first moved in, Chanel didn't see anything unusual about Trey. She shrugged off her Aunt's warning. She didn't understand why everyone was reacting the way they were. *I think they are overly paranoid.* In her kitchen, she warmed up her plate. Still thinking about her neighbor and the conversation she had with her aunt, she began to think deeply about Trey. She sort of missed him. She could use the company and give away some of the food her aunt gave her. Her aunt did pack enough food for days. It was enough to share, and Chanel would still have plenty of leftovers. After she made up her mind about sharing food with Trey, she set the plate down on the counter and proceeded out to knock on his door to offer him an official invitation. Chanel opened her front door to find Andrew standing in front of hers.

"oh." Chanel said, startled.

"Oh hey, I was just about to knock on your door again to see if you were free," he started.

"Yes, sure," Chanel replied. She felt a bit uneasy but quickly shook it off. "What's up?"

"I wanted to know where you free again this week to hang out. I enjoyed your company. I was thinking about you."

"Aww, that's sweet. That's funny because I was thinking about you too and wanted to know if you would be open to some good food my aunt brought?"

"Really?"

"Yes, she brought mac n cheese, greens, sweet potatoes, and honey ham."

"Damn, that sounds good."

"Yea, she packed so much I can share. I could come over now if you want and bring the food over?"

"That sounds like a plan. I would love that."

"Okay, cool." So, Chanel went back into her apartment and grabbed all the plates of food. Trey stood there, waiting to help her bring the food up. 'Oh, were you waiting for me?" Chanel asked sweetly.

"Yes, I didn't want to leave you with all that food to carry by yourself. I don't mind helping." This made Chanel smile. *See, I don't see an ounce of evil in him. Just paranoid.* Together they brought all of the plates of food to Trey's condo. He held the door open for Chanel as she came in. "Thank you, Trey," she said as she stood in his hallway.

"Thanks."

"No problem." he responded.

"Where would you like me to place this?"

"Here," as motioned for her to come into the kitchen and sit it on the counter. As Chanel placed the food down, she felt him brush up behind her. She turned found and found him standing right there.

Chanel immediately turned red.

"Oh, I'm sorry I didn't mean to scare you." He said jokingly. Chanel just looked at him with a blank expression. She was slightly creeped out but also slightly turned on.

"Uhm," Chanel started; as she squeezed past him "what kind of plates do you have?" she asked, trying to change the subject.

"Let's use paper plates because I don't want to wash dishes."

"I don't blame you." Trey reached up and brought down the paper plates for both him and Chanel to use.

He set the plates down next to her. Chanel arranged the dishes in order from wet to dry. "Do you have any utensils that I can use to serve the food?"

"Of course. What would you like a fork or a spoon?"

"Spoon, please." Trey reached down to the drawer beneath him and pulled out two plastic spoons.

"You don't have to work about serving spoons. I don't mind my food being mixed. It's all going to the same place." Trey laughed.

"You shall right," Chanel responded as she joined his laughter. Chanel smiled at the thought of being at Trey's house sharing food with him, communicating, smiling, just enjoying each other's company. Chanel gave Trey larger portions. She remembers her Aunt would say, *"a man needs a lot to eat."* She wanted to make sure it was enough for him.

"Hopefully, this is enough?"

"That's perfect," he responded. Then Chanel served herself last. When she was finished, Trey ushered her to his living room to sit on that sectional. They sat down next to each other. Chanel started praying over her food and ended her prayer. She heard Trey say, "amen."

"Do you believe in God?"

"Yes, I do. I grew up in the church. My dad was a pastor."

"Really?"

"Oh, wow, that's amazing. I bet you know all the bible verses."

"Lol, I know a fair amount," Trey chuckled. They both began to eat their food. The food was so good. Chanel's aunt put her foot in this. Trey started smacking; this food was so good. It wasn't long before they cleared all the food off their plates, and was beyond stuff.

"Well, that was amazing," Trey started.

"I know, my aunt put her foot in that food."

"Heck yea, she did. She cooks like my mom and grandma. Good ole soul-food does the body good," Trey said as he looked at Chanel. He leaned closer and squeezed her knee slightly.

"So, Chanel, what's on your mind?" Chanel felt her face become red. She didn't know how to answer. So she just said,

"Nothing. What about you?"

"Well, I'm sitting next to a lovely young lady to who I'm very attracted too. I enjoy your company. It brings me peace."

"Really?"

"Yes, I look forward to seeing you. You're the perfect end to any day," Trey said as he leaned in closer. "Chanel, I have a favor to ask you?" Trey said with his bedroom eyes

"Uh sure?" she replied

"I know you don't get intimate with men. And I don't want to freak you out. But I couldn't help thinking about you since the last time you were here. You felt so comfortable for me. You enjoyed your presence. You are amazing. I didn't realize how much I missed being in a woman's presence until you showed up in my life. I truly believe that you being here is a gift from God. I've been lonely for some time now, and I miss everything about a woman. From the smell, their touch, their presence, their body," he started. Chanel just looked with a blank expression on her face. She couldn't believe the words that were coming out of his mouth. Only then, he reached out and caressed Chanel's hand and moved closer. Slightly biting his lips, he got up and began to caress Chanel's neck. Chanel felt her body react to his touch.

"Chanel," he continued, "I see the way you look at me. And I know you want me. So I'm just going to go ahead and say it. I want you to consider spending the night with me. Here is my bed. You lay in my arms, and I hold you every night until the sun comes up." Chanel didn't know how to respond or honestly know what he was saying.

"I'm sorry," Chanel began, "can you explain that deeper to me, please?"

"What is there to explain? I want you to spend the night with me; every night. If you like, you can shower here too," Trey said with a steady gaze. Chanel felt stuck. She didn't know how to respond. I barely know him.

"We barely know each other," Chanel began.

"I know; we just met not too long ago. But, I feel sort of an attachment to you. I think it would be good for you. I can see us together," Trey started.

"Uhm, I don't think that's appropriate," she managed to speak out her astonishment. She felt her stomach turn butterflies.

He reached out again, "please, Chanel. I'm a lonely old man who's looking to love someone. I would love for her to be you. You are everything I need. You are smart, beautiful, and talented. Plus, it would help relieve both of us. I'm a pleaser. I'll do anything for you," he said as he bit his lips. Chanel felt uneasy. Just then, her Aunt's words popped into her head. *Is this what she meant by off?* Chanel started feeling all the blood rushing to her face shook her head

"No... no..." she continued shaking her head, "sorry, I can't." She bolted off the couch and headed straight to his door as she began to unlock it.

"Wait, Chanel" he started. But before he could even finish his sentence, Chanel was out the door and onto the steps. She reached her apartment and quickly closed the door behind her. She pressed her back against the door and just stood there.

"Chanel, please open up," she heard Trey from the other side of her door. He started knocking. But Chanel wouldn't budge. Then finally she went into her bedroom and saw she had a missed call from her aunt. Still feeling uneasy and confused, she picked up the phone called her back.

"Hello," her aunt started.

"hey aunt, how are you?" Chanel replied, trying to mask her emotions.

"I'm good, baby yourself?"

"I'm okay," Chanel replied with uncertainty in her voice. Picking up on her niece distress

"what's wrong, baby?" her aunt asked.

"Oh, nothing auntie," Chanel lied. She couldn't tell her that she went over to that man's house after she just warned her about him. But Chanel aunt is smart. Too smart. She knew Chanel was hiding something. So instead of pressing the issue, she simply says

"Chanel, whatever is bothering you, just know you have the power of choice." Chanel instantly felt relief. Her aunt was right. She does have the power of choice.

"Thanks, auntie. I'm glad you made it home safe."

"Yes, I'm glad I got to see you."

"Me too. And I will be definitely over your house soon for a Sunday dinner."

"Yes, that would be lovely. Oh, and make sure you bring your church clothes."

"Uh?"

"Yes, bring your church clothes. I'm taking you to church with me. You know it's been a while since you last came, and everyone asks about how you're doing all the time."

"Okay, auntie." Chanel replied as she rolled her eyes.

"Good night."

"Sleep tight."

"Don't let the bed bugs bite." they said in unison. They both laughed and hung up the phone. Chanel began to regain her composure, and then she heard a knock at the door. Chanel knew it was Trey. She slowly got up from the bed and walked to her front door. When she opened it, Trey was standing there with a perplexed look on his face.

"Hey, I realized I should not have said that to you. I didn't mean to make you feel uncomfortable."

"It's okay. Uhm, about your offer, I will decline. I just don't think it's right. Plus, we are friends."

"I understand," he started, "you left your food over here. Would you like to come to get it?"

"Uhm, sure," Chanel replied. She walked into his apartment and grabbed the plates of food. As she turned around, she found him standing behind her again. This time she could feel his manhood resting against the bottom of her back. She took a deep breath. She quickly turned around and brushed passed him and didn't speak a word. She marched herself down the steps, into her apartment, and kicked the door closed with her foot. She set the food down on the counter and "breathed."

"Chanel." She heard him call her from the hallway. She ignored him. He continued to knock on her door every hour. She just wanted her space and time to reflect. She didn't understand. She already told him no. Why was he always pressing the issue? Plus, she couldn't believe that he was still pushing up on her after she told him no! Chanel decided to ignore his knocking. It was going at 10:00 pm, and Chanel had a class in the morning. So she took a quick shower and hopped into the bed. She laid there, staring at the ceiling until she finally went to sleep.

Prey

Flashback

"Chanel, you feel so wet baby." Andrew moaned in her ear as he fingered her. Chanel moaned back. He pushed his fingers deeper inside her like he was digging for treasure. With his free hand, Andrew pulled his manhood out and began to stroke himself. Out of reflex, Chanel started to stroke him. The two kissed widely in her dorm room. It was daytime, and everyone was out at the annual picnic. Chanel and Andrew snuck away to her dorm room mess around. Andrew started taking Chanel's clothes off. This isn't the first time they got utterly naked during an intense kissing session. After Andrew finished taking off her clothes, he then took off his. Now the two were completely naked in her bed as they laid in a spoon position. Feeling risker, Andrew started rubbing the head of his penis near Chanel's opening. Feeling alarmed, Chanel bolted straight up,

"Uhm, no sex," she said.

"I know," he replied, "I'm not going to do anything to you. I just like feeling it on there. You know, baby, I won't do anything to make you feel uncomfortable." He replied as he looked Chanel in the eye as he continued to stroke himself. Still feeling uneasy, she eyed him. She and Andrew have been down this road plenty of times before. They would have a really intense kissing session, with lots of foreplay, oral sex, and never penetration. Chanel still felt uneasy. Andrew sat up and began small kisses on Chanel's back and neck. He leaned closer to her and whispered in her ear, "come lay down baby." Feeling a bit of the tension leave her body, she laid back down and started ago messing around with Andrew. It wasn't long before they were deep in their kisses. Andrew then laid on his back and motioned for Chanel to get on top as if she was riding. That was her favorite. She liked the idea of being in control. She's seen lots of porn with women hanging their men and making them come. She would do that with Andrew one day. As Chanel straddled Andrew, she felt his manhood resting near her clitoris. Andrew was large. His veins popped out, trailing to the head of his penis. The head was vast and meaty. Chanel began to rub herself on him. This felt so good to her. Andrew guided her hips in the rocking motion. He bit his lips as he felt Chanel's womanhood rub her juices all over him. But Andrew; wanted more.

To be honest, Andrew always wanted more. He was wanted sex. He felt he deserved sex. He thought he was a good boyfriend; why can't he have sex with his girlfriend. He wanted Chanel's body. He wanted to feel her. He was tired of this, "kid s***," he wanted the real thing. So Andrew reached down and again; rubbed the head of his penis at Chanel's opening. Chanel froze and watched

Andrew rub his penis head. Eyeing Chanel, Andrew tried pushing the tip of the head in just a bit; Chanel winced and jumped off.

"Andrew, no sex. Please," she said as she stood near the side of the bed. Andrew scoffed.

"I know, baby. You tell me all the time. Trust me, I know," he replied, annoyed. Chanel started to get a funny feeling in her stomach. Something wasn't right about this session. It seemed; off.

"I think we should stop." Chanel said, looking down. Andrew got pissed and sat up.

"Why?" he asked as he looked Chanel full in the face. Chanel became uncomfortable. She didn't like having to explain herself. *Why can't he just respect that I don't want to do this anymore?*

"So, it's okay if you want to rub and kiss, but I can't rub the head of my d*** on yo p****?" Andrew demanded.

"That's not fair Andrew." Chanel pleaded.

"What's not fair? You act like I'm some sort of rapist or something. Chanel, have I done anything to you?" Chanel shook her head. "Exactly. So, I'm not sure as to why you are treating me this way. All I'm doing is rubbing the head of my dick on yo' p****. There's no harm in that. You need to relax and just chill. You're making this bigger than what it needs to be," Andrew huffed. Chanel started to feel guilty. She liked Andrew, and he was haven't done anything to her or disrespect any of her wishes, so she thought. Maybe I do need to relax. Still feeling wrong about Andrew's feelings, Chanel apologized,

"I'm sorry, Andrew. I didn't mean to make you feel like that," she started. "It's just that, I didn't like that you were sticking and rubbing your head so close to being inside me. Maybe, I'm overreacting."

"Yea, I understand, but you need to remember I've never done anything to you that has put you in harm's way. I've been a good boyfriend. You just need to relax and let me finish loving on you." he said with a small grin. Chanel still looked down. She always felt like crap. She didn't want Andrew to feel as if he was the bad guy. At the same time, she even didn't like that he kept putting his head right there. Andrew got off the bed and approached Chanel. He palmed her face and gently kissed her lips.

"Baby, you can trust me," he said in between kisses, "I won't take you too fast. The two started slow dancing in the middle of the floor. Andrew grabbed Chanel by the hand and led her back to the bed. Chanel laid down on her back, and Andrew got on top. Chanel still felt ultra-guilty. Noticing a change in her demeanor, Andrew said, "I know something that will cheer you up." Andrew made a trail of small kisses down Chanel's chest, stopping at her breast and lightly squeezing her nipples with his teeth; he then traveled down to her navel and swirled around with his tongue; he then traveled down to her womanhood and parted her lips with his two fingers. He began kisses, Chanel, in her sweet spot. She moaned. Andrew started licking her clit and fingering her with the other hand. Chanel felt delighted. She began to relax as Andrew performed oral sex on her. As he fingered her deeply, Chanel opened her legs wider. She loved her when his fingers made love to her. It felt so good. Andrew pushed her legs up and started thrusting his tongue inside of Chanel. Chanel felt herself get ready to come. Andrew came back up and started widely kissing her. The two of their tongues began a new language, a new voyage, a discovery. Chanel was so enthralled with the kissing that she didn't see Andrew positioning himself on top of her. As he kissed Chanel, he started fingering her to make her wet.

"Andrew, that feels so good." Chanel moaned. Andrew was silent. He started kissing Chanel's neck as he fingered her. Chanel leaned her head back and closed her eyes. She then felt Andrew's head near her opening. She slightly tensed up. Then she remembered that Andrew said he would never hurt her and that she can trust him. He just likes to feel her opening. So she relaxed, believing that she can trust him. As she furthered relaxed, her trust for Andrew will soon be torn to shreds.

Andrew wanting more from Chanel and tired of the "kid s***," thrust his penis inside Chanel and began rapping her.

Chanel froze in disbelief. Her body tensed up, and she didn't say anything. Andrew worked his way back to her lips and started kissing her as he continued raping her.

"See, baby," he said in-between kisses, "I told you there's nothing to worry about. Don't this feel good, baby. Damn, this feels good," he moaned. Chanel was frozen. She didn't know how to respond. She couldn't believe that after all that, he still went against her wishes. Chanel felt herself get sick. Chanel was deep inside her mind. She didn't realize that she disconnected from the trauma that she was experiencing and found a safe space in her mind to be. She started thinking of her childhood and how wonderful it was. She remembered going fishing with her uncle every summer at lake Kross, where they would fish for catfish. When Andrew finished, that's when she came too. Andrew sat on the side of the bed and looked down at Chanel.

"That was amazing, baby. You felt so good. I loved f****** you. I can't wait to do it again," he said as he caressed her thigh. Chanel still froze didn't say anything. She just had a look. She was afraid, confused, and unsure. Do I say something? She questioned herself. But when she opened her mouth, the words escaped her. Andrew misinterpreting her body language, said, "I know baby. I would be speechless too," he joked. Chanel tried to make herself laugh. But no. She couldn't. She couldn't do anything at the moment. It was like her body shut down. Unknowingly, she sat on the side of her bed. She looked down and traced the floor lines with her eyes. She then looked up at the pictures on her desk. It was pictures of her mother, dad, grandmother, and aunt.

Andrew stood up off the bed and said, "We need some lights in here." So he walked over to the switch and turned it on. When he came back, his face turned white. Chanel looked down and saw all the blood on her covers. She looked up at him one more time and blacked out.

"Earth to Chanel," her classmate said. "earth to Chanel. Hello, are you there?" Chanel focused back on her classmate's face. She realized she must have zoned out. "Hey," was all she could manage to say. "What's wrong, honey?" her classmate asked. Chanel took a deep breath, "let's walk." Both ladies left their books, notebooks, pencils, and paper at the table and headed outside. The air was cold. The sun-kissed Chanel's gorgeous ebony brown skin. She wore a yellow sundress that complimented her skin and a high bun. They walked a distance before Chanel finally told her what was bothering her.

"What would you do if a man is asking you to spend the night with him?" Chanel asked.

"Hmm, are you guys having sex?" her classmate asked.

"Nah, all he wants to do is cuddle."

"Idk, it doesn't seem too bad. How old is he?"

"He's 35."

"You definitely wanna be careful since he's an older man. You never know the tricks they got up their sleeve."

"True."

"How well do you know him?"

"I'm getting to know him. He's my neighbor, and he lives upstairs from me. He comes off as really nice and attentive. I think he's just lonely."

"Yea, that's typical for men his age. Does he have any kids?"

"Not that I know of."

"Well, I don't think it's too bad of an idea to spend the night with him. Just as long as you don't have sex with him, it's cool."

"You right."

"Yea, if he wants some c******, he needs to be paying a bill or two." Both ladies chuckled. "I'm a serious, girl. The c****** is not free!"

"Thanks, girl, I appreciate that, a lot!"

"No problem, hun." Both ladies walked back towards the building.

"And if he really cute," her classmate started, "find out if he has a brother." Both ladies laughed in unison. "Girl, you crazy," they said as they walked into the building.

Chanel sat down in her spot and started back working. She felt a weight leave off her chest. She began to think about Trey. I might talk with him about his offer Chanel thought to herself. It was about 12:30 pm, and Chanel was hungry. She worked tirelessly on her research paper about neuroscience and cognitive function in relation to physical fitness.

"I think; I'm going to head out, pick me up some lunch, and go home and nap for a couple of hours," Chanel said as she started to gather up her things.

"Yea girl, me too."

"Yea! Thanks for helping me today with that situation."

'No problem, honey. Don't forget what I told you."

"Of course." Chanel smiled, "no sex."

"Right!" Both ladies laughed as they continued to pack up their stuff. Once finished, they headed to their cars.

"Alright, girl," Chanel said as she reached her car. "Talk to you later. We should link up again."

"yes, girl. This was much needed. Don't hesitate to call or text."

"Alright," Chanel said as she entered her car. She started her car and waited for her classmate to pull off first. Then she followed shortly after. She stopped by Chick-fil-a on the way home. After purchasing her food and pulling through the drive-thru she got a call from her aunt. Chanel quickly put her food to the side. Fumbling the phone, she hurried up and connected it to the Bluetooth in her car.

"Hello," Chanel said as she pulled off.

"Hey baby, how are you?"

"I'm good, auntie, yourself?"

"I'm doing good, baby. Just wanted to check-in. I haven't spoken to you in a few days."

"Yea, I know. I've been super busy with school and work. I haven't forgotten about your plans for church and Sunday dinner."

"oh, baby, I ain't worried about that. I figured once you get some time free in your schedule, then we will hang out."

"Of course."

"So, anything new going on in your life?" Chanel's aunt asked. That threw Chanel for a loop. She knows her aunt will not just say something like that off the hump.

"No, nothing new or exciting." Chanel lied. She didn't want to tell her aunt that she went over to that man's house after warning her not to get involved with him.

"Okay. Well, you know yall young folks have so much adventure in yall life. It's way different from when I was coming up. But, I like that you all have this new freedom. It's in developing who you are."

"This is true, auntie" Chanel replied. She had just pulled in front of her condo. But she waited to exit the car.

"Okay, honey. I didn't want anything. Be safe, okay, and remember, Chanel; life is all about choices. Make good choices." Her aunt said. Chanel nodded her head and said, "yes, ma'am." She hung up the phone and sat in her car for a while. *I wonder what made her say that?* Chanel sat in her car and started eating her food. She ate in silence. Then her thoughts slowly drifted to Trey. She wondered what he was doing. She looked at his patio window and didn't see any sign of him in the house. He must be at work, Chanel concluded. Well, when he gets here, I'll talk with him. She felt herself get ultra-excited. She missed Trey, honestly. She hasn't spoken to him in a few days since their last conversation. She was upset with him pushing himself on her, and she wasn't entirely sure about the whole spending the night thing. She liked Trey, and she welcomed his friendship. But she didn't like the cost associated with it. Chanel finished eating her food and checked her watch. The time was 1:07 pm. Perfect, just enough time for a quick nap and then back off to sell some hair.

Chanel exited her car and walked into her condo building. She dropped her book bag at the door. She walked into the bathroom and took a quick pee. She washed up and headed to bed. She laid in her bed, thinking about Trey. *I can't wait to see him.*

Chanel woke up to a loud banging at her door. *Whose that?* Still sleepy, she positioned herself on the edge of the bed, letting her feet dangle. She clenched the edge of the bed, and rocked back and forth. She did this for five minutes until she finally pushed herself off. A little dizzy, she gained her balanced and walked to the front door. She couldn't tell who it was standing in the hallway. Then another loud bang. "Okay, okay, hold on, please." When she opened the door, she found Trey standing right there.

"So you are just going to ignore me?" he shouted at her.

"Huh?" Chanel replied with a puzzled look on her face.

"You heard me. So you're just going to ignore me. I knocked on your door all night?" Trey continued to shout at Chanel. Chanel started to feel embarrassed. She didn't want the other neighbors to hear them arguing.

"Uhm, can we continue this conversation maybe inside?" she asked calmly.

"Nah," Trey spat at her. "I thought you were different," he continued. "You could have at least opened the door. But nah, I'm good on you". Chanel was confused. *Why is he acting like that? He's acting like I did something terrible to him.* Chanel was in disbelief. *Is this the same Trey she liked? The gentleman who shared his food with her. So caring. So thoughtful. It couldn't be.* He was acting like that. So Chanel walked into her apartment and closed the door. She starred at Trey through the peephole. He glared at her door before going back upstairs to his condo. Chanel felt sick. She laid her head against the door and took three deep breaths.

Flashes back:

"Chanel, Chanel! Can you hear me?" she heard a voice say over her. She shook her head.

"Uh?" she replied, dizzy.

"Chanel," the voice said again. This time was tugging her arm. Then all of a sudden, she felt cold water all over her face. She sat up. Still dizzy and confused. Through her dizziness, she could Andrew standing right there looking her over.

"Chanel, baby, are you okay?" Chanel didn't respond. She felt sick and lightheaded.

'I just want to lay down?" Chanel tried to lay in the bed.

"I don't think that's a good idea," Andrew said. He tried to stop Chanel from lying down. Chanel put her hand on the bed, and felt something wet between her fingers.

"What's that?" she said as she looked down. She saw it was blood and she freaked out.

"Is this blood?" she asked, scared. "What happened?" Then instantly, she remembered. With the little energy she had, she pushed her up to her feet and moved away from Andrew.

"What's wrong?" he said as he tried to come closer.

"Don't touch me!" she screamed.

"Why are you screaming?" he replied with a puzzled look.

"You know why," she said back, trying to keep her balance. Chanel almost tipped over, and Andrew reached out to try and help her. She immediately pushed his arms away.

"Don't touch me," she screamed.

"Man, you tripping. At least let me help you," he said.

"No, you've done enough." She said.

"What?" Andrew replied with a puzzled look on his face. "What are you talking about?" he responded.

"You know what happened. You raped me!"

"I what?"

"You raped me! You just stuck your penis inside me."

"Man, you let me; you didn't stop me. Nor did you push me off you!" he shouted back.

"I didn't let you do anything. You said that you like just like sticking your head there. I didn't tell you to stick it in."

"Okay, but you still let me. You didn't stop me. And you were moaning." Chanel felt confused. *Did I let him have sex with me? Why didn't I tell him to stop if I didn't want to?* While Chanel tried to sort things out. Andrew said, "man, I'm out of here. You accusing me of rape when you know damn well you wanted it." Chanel shot her head up and looked Andrew thoroughly in the eyes as he continued his tirade against her.

"Yea, you wanted it. We always playing clothes burn and kissing and stuff. You got naked. And you were rubbing yo p**** all on my d***. Everybody knows when you do stuff like that, it automatically leads to sex. Idk what world you live in." Still, Chanel was quiet. She was trying to process everything.

"Man, I'm out of here. This relationship is over. All I ever wanted was to have sex with my girlfriend. Everyone else is having, sex and we can't. We can do anything you want to do, but we can't do anything I want. Then we have sex, and you say I raped you! Please! You liked it. I saw the way you were looking at me during it. You didn't even say stop. If you wanted me to stop, why didn't you just say it?!?! Bye, Chanel, you're delusional." Andrew, who was already dressed grabbed his phone, wallet, and charger. He turned and looked back at Chanel one more time before leaving her alone in her dorm room left to face the reality that he created for them.

Chanel started crying. She hugged her nude body closely and rocked back and forth. Her suitemate had just walked in and heard Chanel crying. Knocking on the door,

"Chanel are you okay?" she asked. The door slightly opened. Andrew didn't close the door tightly. Unexpectedly, the suitemate just walked in and found Chanel crying half-naked with blood all over her covers. Her suitemate immediately rushed over to her. With panic in her voice, she said,

"Chanel, are you okay? What happened? Who did this to you?" But all Chanel could do was cry.

Chanel lifts her head off the door. She adjusted her clothes and fixed her hair. She took a deep breath and walked back into her bedroom. She sat down on her bed and cried. She couldn't believe Trey was acting like that. After several minutes of crying, she finally decided that it was time to get up and head to school. She had a class and some studying to do. She got up off the bed, used the bathroom, brushed her teeth, fixed her hair, and straightened her clothes. She walked back into her bedroom and retrieved her phone and wallet. Her bookbag sat near the door already setup to go from earlier. She grabbed her bag and pulled her keys out of the side pocket. Chanel opened her condo door and stepped into the hallway. It was quiet. She looked up the steps. She briefly thought about Trey and their altercation. I'll talk to him later, she thought. She walked outside and headed towards her car. A few neighbors were out. She wondered if they heard the argument between Trey and her. She quickly let the thought leave her mind. Chanel unlocked her car door and sat inside. She sat all of her belongings on the passenger seat next to her. She started her car and backed out of her parking spot cautiously, and looked over her shoulders to make sure there were no cars behind her. She drove out of the parking lot and headed for school. On the way there, she played the radio to help ease her mind before walking into the library. She didn't want today's drama to hinder her. Chanel was lucky that the school was so close to her new home. Driving there was a breeze. She made it to the school and moved into the parking garage. She found a spot near the elevator on the second floor. She parked her car and grabbed all of the materials that she needed for the day. Chanel exited her car, locked it, and proceeded to the elevator. Once inside the elevator, she pressed the 5th floor because that's bridge exit. She leaned her head against the wall. She closed her eyes and felt pressure building up. She was beginning to have a migraine. Starting to feel nauseous she closed her nose, and started deep breathing. Then the elevator chimed, and the doors opened. She opened her eyes and saw she made it to the bridge. Chanel walked towards the campus and saw one of her classmates standing on the bridge.

"Hey girl," her classmate spoke as she waved at Chanel.

"Hey girl," she replied. She was trying to mask the confusion in her voice.

"How are things going?"

"Things are going good. Did you complete that chem quiz online?"

'Yes, girl that dang on quiz was hard."

"Yes, tell me about it. It was extremely difficult"

"Where are you headed?"

"The library. You?"

"I'm heading to the cafeteria. You should come?"

"Aw, thanks, I appreciate that a lot." Chanel thought about going to the library. Then again, she could use something to drink. "Sure, I'll come"

"Awesome," her classmate replied. Both ladies walked to the cafeteria together.

"So how are your other classes going?" her classmate asked.

"They're going good. No complaints. I'm not taking as many classes this semester. Plus, I'm almost done"

"Really?"

"Yes, ma'am. I took classes over the summer, and I when I was a freshman, I did the Bridge program where I did college courses at a high school level."

"Dang, girl, you smart as hell." Both ladies laughed in unison.

"Girl, I can't wait to be done."

"When do you graduate?"

"May"

"Oh, girl, that's next semester. You can do it."

"Yes, girl. I can't let anything mess me up! Almost at the finish line."

"I'm super happy for you," her classmate replied. By this time, they made it to the escalator and took them down to the lower level to reach the restaurant. The smell of chicken fingers and French fries filled the air. Both ladies entered the cafeteria. As Chanel's classmate ordered food while she bought a bottle of water. Chanel waited as her classmate waited until her food was done. She followed her classmate to a booth near the window.

"What do you have to work on?"

"Today, I'm working on my biochemistry assignment."

"Dang, you take biochem and chem. Whew, girl, you are a trooper because those are hard classes."

"Girl, tell me about it. I don't know what I thought when I decided to take both of them together."

"You wasn't"

"Girl, you ain't never lied," Chanel replied. She started to feel so much better. She opened her bottle of water and started to feel relief. Then this strange feeling began to wash over her. It was like sinking in the bottom of her stomach. She suddenly felt someone was watching her. Trying to shake the feeling, she ignored it. *That's just your nerves, girl. Nobody is watching you,* she told herself. In an attempt to convince herself it was all in her head, she surveyed the cafeteria. Nothing seemed out of the ordinary. Everyone was enjoying their food. *See it's all in your head.* That's when Chanel stomach dropped. On the second level near the escalator, she found Trey watching her. She choked on her drink.

'What's wrong? Are you okay?" The classmate asked.

"Yea, I'm fine." Chanel replied as she cleared her throat. She took a long sip of her water. When Chanel looked over again, Trey was gone. Chanel felt a cold chill run down her spine. What is he doing here? Did he follow me here? Chanel felt too sick to finish drinking her water. So instead, she tried to focus on her work. Her classmate noticed how different she became.

"Are you sure everything is okay, Chanel?"

"I will be." Suddenly, Chanel bolted up and threw her water away, and gathered her belongings. Chanel was highly disturbed. Her classmate looked confused.

"Hey, girl. I realized that I needed to do something significant. I'll catch you later."

"okay," her classmate said with a puzzled look on her face. Chanel made her way to the escalator, and hurriedly walked towards the bridge. When she made it to the elevator, she pushed the down button. *What is happening today?* When the elevator opened, Trey was standing there.

Chanel gasped.

"Hey Chanel," he said in a guilty tone.

"Uhm, hey? What are you doing here? Did you follow me?" she asked. Trey, with small hesitation in his voice, answered, "yes." Chanel was floored. *Why on earth would this mad follow her to school. Is he crazy?*

"Are you crazy?" Chanel asked.

"No," he responded softly.

"Well, what are you doing here?" Chanel demanded.

"Well, I felt bad about what happened earlier. I wanted to apologize to you. But you left so fast. I saw you leaving from my patio window."

"Trey, you can't just go around following people."

"I know; I didn't think. I reacted. I'm sorry, Chanel, I didn't mean to hurt you. I care very deeply about you." Chanel wasn't convinced.

"Well…"

'Well, what?" he said.

"Well, apologize. I want to hear it," Chanel said in a stern tone. Trey looked Chanel over and saw she was serious.

"Chanel, I'm sorry I over-reacted. I had no right to talk to you that way. I truly do value our friendship. I think you are something special. What I said was wrong. Can you forgive me?" he asked. Chanel thought about it for a second.

"I guess," she replied.

"Nah, I don't want you to guess; I want you to know," Trey said.

"Oh, and another thing," Trey added.

"Yes," Chanel said.

"I would not have had to act that way if you opened the door."

"Wait; what?"

"Yea, if you would have just opened the door and said something, I would not have acted like that. You have some fault there too."

"Uhm, no, I don't."

"Yes, you do."

"I don't owe you an explanation. Suppose I don't feel like talking at the moment. I needed some space."

"Well, if you just said that, I would have understood."

"Wow, so you're blaming me."

"I'm not blaming you for anything. Just letting you know what's facts. Communication is a two-way street. Accountability works both ways," Trey said as he studied Chanel's face.

"Nah, I'm not apologizing for that. You're the one you went off on me, and you followed me to school, and you're pretty much blaming me for your behavior. You are the only one who can control how you act. The responsibility falls on you."

"Wow."

"Look, Chanel, I don't want to debate with you. I just want to make sure our friendship isn't over," Trey replied.

"Sure, it's not over," she said back.

"Okay. Oh, can I ask you for one more favor?" he asked.

"Yea, what's that?"

"Can I have a hug? I could use one." Chanel made a face at his request. *He wants me to hug him.*

"It's just a simple hug. Nothing special. I just want to seal our friendship with a hug, if that's okay," he said as he cracked a smile. Chanel was still a little hesitant. She rolled her eyes and walked towards him. Trey opened his arms and went to embrace Chanel. Chanel gave him a quick hug and retrieved back quickly.

"Uhm, what was that?" Trey asked.

"A hug," Chanel responded.

"Nah, that wasn't a hug. That was one of them church hugs. I want a real hug." Chanel winced. She really didn't want to hug this man.

"You act like I'm going to harm you. It's just a hug," Trey said. "I promise; I won't go overboard." Chanel wanted to believe him. She took a deep breath and stepped towards Trey again. This time when they embraced, the hug lasted much longer. His body felt warm and firm against her frame. She smelled his cologne, and he smelled amazing. She found herself in a trance. This man felt so good. She could stay in his arms forever. She felt Trey's hands as he caressed her back. When Chanel let go and returned to her side of the elevator, she saw Trey smile at her.

"See, was it that bad?" he asked with a smirk.

"Nah, it wasn't," Chanel said. She was too busy looking down at her watch to notice that Trey has moved to her side of the elevator. When she looked up again, Trey was in front of her. He gently grabbed Chanel's chin and pulled her face closer to his. Trey planted his soft lips on Chanel's. Chanel was in shock. *Is this man kissing me?* Chanel pulled her face back. Trey looked Chanel in her eyes and bit his lips, "Chanel, I like you a lot. I wish you would reconsider spending the night at my house with me." Chanel didn't know how to respond. She was still in shock from the kiss she received from Trey.

"Uhm, Trey, I am extremely flattered, but I'm not sure yet. I just don't think it will be a good idea."

"What makes you say that?"

"Well, because we barely know each other. Plus, you're so much older than me. How do I know you're not trying to manipulate me or will take advantage of me?"

"Well, you have my word. I won't do anything to harm you."

"I don't know if that is enough."

"Chanel, have I done anything to you that has made you feel uncomfortable?" he asked.

"Yes, you followed me to school." She responded.

"You know what, that was a bad question?" Trey chuckled. "Besides that?

"No, not really," she responded.

"See, you have nothing to worry about. It's all in that beautiful head of yours. Just trust me." Trey said.

"Well, I still need to think about it," Chanel responded.

"Well, just let me know. I'll be waiting. Okay."

"Oh, I just remembered, you did do something that made me uncomfortable. When you brushed up on me that day in your apartment. I didn't like that. That's the reason why I wasn't answering my door. I didn't feel like explaining to you why it made me feel uncomfortable."

"Understood."

"I'll try my best not to do that. Idk how successful I will be. I am a man."

"And what does that mean?" Chanel questioned.

"It means, it's in my nature. As I said, I will try my best." Chanel didn't like his answer. *Like he will try his best. That sounds like a cop-out.* Chanel couldn't believe his behavior and commentary sometimes. She just rolled her eyes. She looked down at her watch and saw the time. *I really need to study.*

"Okay, Trey, I'll catch you later. I have studied that I need to accomplish."

"I understand. Will I see you tonight?"

"Yea, there's a possibility."

"Okay." The elevator door opened and she stepped out. She watched as Trey pushed for his floor and the doors closed. She let her thoughts linger a bit longer. There is truly something about this man. Chanel turned and headed towards the library. She figured she had an hour to study before her class starts.

After her class ended, she looked down at the time. It was 4:30 pm. *I think I can head home now. I'm beat.* Chanel was exhausted. She a long day. School, work, Trey. Just the thought of his name made her excited. She walked towards the elevator. Once inside, she pressed for the 3rd floor. Off the elevator, she went and started walking towards her car. She began to think about the possibility of sleeping over at Trey's house tonight. His body felt so good against hers, and she would be lying if she said she didn't want to touch him again. She wanted him that bad. At her car, she chirped the lock and got in. Once inside, she began her ritual of sitting her items in the passenger seat, adjusting herself in the mirror, starting the car, looking behind her to make sure it was safe to pull out, and proceeded on her way. On the ride home, Chanel let her mind take her to different places. She wondered what it felt like to sleep in Trey's bed, to feel his lips against hers, his body near hers, his hands, everything. She was so enthralled with her fantasies; she barely paid attention to the road. *Pay attention, girl. You got this man all up in your head.* Then the words of her aunt came into play. Make good choices. Chanel felt stuck. She knew she better not get involved with that man; but she was very interested.

Trey seemed like a nice man. He seemed like he cared for her and wouldn't do anything to hurt her. She didn't understand why so many people felt he was a "bad guy." He didn't seem like a bad guy to her. He seemed like a nice older man. Chanel finally arrived at her condo. She saw Trey standing outside on his patio. He was smiling, talking to another neighbor. Chanel got a little nervous. *I hope he doesn't bring any attention to me.* Chanel looked herself over in the mirror again. *I look good!* She exited the car, and just as she assumed, Trey brought attention to her.

"Well, hello, college scholar. How was class?" he asked from his patio. The other neighbor, a young man from up the street, looked over at Chanel and smiled. She smiled back at this neighbor and answered Trey with a grin, "Class was great. I did lots of studying and feel accomplished".

"What you go to school for," the neighbor asked Chanel.

"I go for biochemistry."

"Oh word, you must be made smart. I attend college myself."

"Really? What school?"

"I currently go to community college. I'm studying radiology."

"Oh, that's dope! So you use those x-rays to look inside people's bodies."

"Yea. I can't wait to get started, though. I just started the program this fall."

"Oh, wow, congrats. I heard you guys have to apply for before actually starting."

"Yes, we do. Which I was a little annoyed with because I felt I should be able to get in, especially if I'm doing all the prereqs."

"Heck yea, you should. I feel you on that." Chanel was so occupied with her conversation with her younger neighbor that she didn't see Trey go back inside.

"So how old are you if don't mind me asking?" he asked.

"I'm 19 years old."

"Oh word, I'm 21." He replied. Chanel looked at her younger neighbor over. He was very handsome. Dark skin, with a low cut, dimples, a full goatee, a little stocky, medium height 5'8', white teeth.

"Oh, really?"

"Yea really." He replied with a smirk.

"So, you got a job?" he asked.

"Yes, I sale weave part-time, and I work at an insurance call center."

"Oh word, that's what's up. So you got two jobs, go to school, educated, and very beautiful if I might add," her neighbor finished. Chanel blushed. At that moment, Trey was standing outside glaring at Chanel. The younger neighbor noticed Trey's demeanor and how he was looking at Chanel.

"Yo' my bad, I didn't mean to overstep," her neighbor said, holding his hands up. Chanel looked at the outer door and saw Trey standing there.

"Nah, it's cool young blood," Trey responded. Chanel felt guilty. *What was I thinking?* Chanel looked away. The younger neighbor feeling uncomfortable, started walking towards his condo. As he walked away from her doubled back and said,

"Nice meeting you," as he looked in Chanel's direction. Chanel smiled and responded, "nice meeting you too. As soon as he was out of earshot Trey said, "aw, you got you a new boyfriend now, huh?"

"Nah, it's not even like that. We were just talking, you know. Nothing serious."

"You sure? I saw how he was looking at you, smiling all in your face. You are smiling back. Is that what you like?"

"No. I mean, he's nice looking, but it was a harmless conversation."

"Nice looking. So you think he looks better than me?"

"No, I didn't say that at all. Why are you acting like this?"

"Acting like what? I'm just asking questions." By this time, Chanel had enough. She was tired. She was hungry. And she didn't have time for his bullcrap."Look, Trey; I'm going in. I'm exhausted, plus hungry. We can talk later if you like?" Chanel started walking towards the door. As she grabbed the handle, Trey put his hand on top of hers, "are you coming over to sleep tonight?" he asked. Chanel looked Trey in the eyes. *What do I say?* Before she could even answer her, Trey got an attitude. "See, this is what I'm talking about."

"Huh?" Chanel responded.

"Yea, I wanna make you mines and you were playing. But it's okay for you to flirt with other men in my face."

"Trey, I don't know what you are talking about. You didn't even give me a chance to answer. You just assumed that I would say no. That's not fair."

"Bull****," he spat in her face. Chanel became fearful.

"What is up with you. You've been aggressive these past few days. Is everything okay?"

"Yea, everything will be. Just forget. Just forget that I ever asked you to spend the night with me." Trey removed his hand from hers. Chanel was stunned. She looked at Trey in complete amazement. Chanel waited to see if he would say something. But no, he just looked in the other direction as if she wasn't there. Still shocked, Chanel grabbed the handle and walked into her condo building. She unlocked her front door and walked in. She immediately ran to her bed and threw herself on the ground. She couldn't believe how Trey was acting. Just in complete shock. Still feeling confused, Chanel texted her friend Courtney.

"Hey, girl," Chanel typed. Courtney did not respond right away. So Chanel got herself situated. While waiting for Courtney's reply, she took off her clothes and used the toilet. She ran a hot shower. Inside the shower, she just let the hot water roll down her back, butt, legs, thighs, hair. Etc. The shower was soothing to her soul. She felt at peace. Chanel started thinking about today's events with Trey, from the stalking at school, the kiss, and his anger in talking to other men. *Maybe, it's men. Perhaps I should just give him what he wants. Then she thought, wait, he's not my man. Why do I owe him anything! It's not like we are together; he is my neighbor.* Chanel was conflicted. She hated that Trey was upset with her; at the same time, she didn't like how he was acting. Decisions, decisions. Chanel continued her shower. She didn't wash her body; she just let the waterfall all over her. This was the first time she's been able to relax somewhat. She just needed time to think about the choice she was going to make. She initially told Trey no to his offer. However, he's persistent. She felt genuinely stuck between doing what's right and standing up for herself or giving into Trey. Chanel finished her shower. She exited her steaming bathroom and laid out on her bed, naked. She saw that Courtney had texted her, but she was interrupted by a knock at the door. Chanel got up, still naked, and looked through the peephole. It was Trey. She rolled her eyes.

"Yes," she answered through the door.

"Hey, Chanel, can we talk?"

"Hold on please," Chanel went and grabbed her robe. It was too long and thick. It was one of those old skool robes that a grandma usually wears. She opened the door and felt the cold air from the hallway kiss her cheeks.

"Oh, sorry. I didn't realize you were busy," he said as he eyed Chanel.

"Yea, I was taking a shower. What's up?"

"Can I step in for a moment?"

"Sure." Chanel opened her door wider and let Trey in. She stepped over to the side while he stood near the door.

"It looks nice in here," he said, trying to make small talk.

"Thanks," Chanel said very dryly.

"Are you mad at me?"

"I wouldn't say mad. I'm just trying to sort things out."

"Sort out what?"

"I'm trying to sort out whether or not to spend the night with you? It's tough to navigate."

"Oh. I wanted to talk to you about that?"

"Oh, what about it?"

"I decided that you don't have to. I don't want to make you feel guilty. So, I decided you don't have to."

"Okay, thank you for that. I appreciate that."

"Oh, I'm not finished."

"Oh… I'm sorry," *there's more?* Chanel thought.

"Yea, I wanted also to say we can cool out on our friendship. I just don't want you to feel guilty about being my friend. I want someone who genuinely wants to be my friend and someone who genuinely will appreciate me in general." Chanel was shocked and confused.

"Trey, what are you talking about?"

"I'm talking about our friendship. I feel like it's a little one-sided."

"How is it one-sided. We just became friends. I'm still learning about you. We are still learning from each other. We have small disagreements here and there, but this is a bit extreme."

"It's not extreme. I care about you, and I want to get to know you more. But you keep having me wait. This is what I don't understand, and I saw how you were talking to that boy. So maybe it would be better if you hung out with that boy instead," Trey finished.

"Trey, you are making way bigger than what this needs to be. I don't understand. I feel like you are trying to control me. It's like whenever I don't do something you want, you get mad."

"I'm not trying to control you."

"In a way, you are. First, you got mad at me for not answering my door, after you made me feel uncomfortable. Now you're unfriending me because I haven't decided yet to spend the night. I mean, what is the big deal?"

"I'm susceptible, Chanel. I just want to be around you. I just want to be near you. And you won't let me."

"I said I need to make up my mind. Can I please make up my mind?"

"Okay, I'll let you make up your mind. Maybe this might help." Trey stepped towards Chanel and wrapped his massive arms around her small body. He just held her in his arms. Chanel, a little startled, said, "Uhm, what are you doing?"

"Shhh," Trey responded. He then started kissing her neck and caressing her back. Chanel felt herself become moist. "Uhm Trey," she murmured. He continued to kiss her neck. He removed his hands from around her robe and stuck them underneath. His hands felt her warm naked body. Chanel jumped. Trey pulled back. "You're naked?" he said.

"Uhm, yea, I was just in the shower before you knocked."

"Mmmm," he moaned. "May I?" he said as he motioned to take off her robe. Chanel made a face.

Trey raised his brow. As he pulled away, Chanel finally answered, "yea," very uneasy.

Trey looked Chanel in her eyes, "are you sure?" he said.

"Yes," she replied. Trey smiled. He took Chanel by the hand and led her to her bedroom. In there, they stood in the middle of the floor. Trey began to undo Chanel's robe as it fell to the floor. He licked his lips. Chanel just stood there. She didn't know how to respond. She's never been with a man this much older than her. She was a little frightened.

"Don't be a scared baby," Trey said as if he can read her thoughts. He pulled Chanel's naked body towards him and started kissing her all over. He first started at her neck as he coupled her breast. As he massaged her nipples with his thumbs, he made a small trail of kisses down her neck to her small petite breast. He kneeled down and starting sucking her nipples very softly. Chanel's body exploded.

His tongue was so soft. He felt so good against her hardened nipples. As Trey continued to suck her nipples, he removed his hand from one of her breasts and made his way down to her vagina. There he played with her and felt her wetness on his fingertips. Chanel moaned. Trey moaned back. Trey pushed Chanel towards her bed. She fell over when she felt the bed hit the back of her legs. She laid down, and Trey opened her legs. He bent over and licked her navel. He gently flicked his tongue as a way to tease her. Andrew smelled Chanel womanhood and became more excited by the smell. He began to tongue kiss the clitoris very passionately. Chanel felt a shiver up her spine, and her thighs slightly tremble. She looked down to see Trey looking back up at her. He parted her lips and slid his tongue into her vaginal opening. Chanel gasped. Chanel moaned in ecstasy. She couldn't believe she was letting this older man perform oral sex on her. Just then, Trey stopped.

"Come back to my place," Trey said as he stood up to face Chanel. Chanel looked puzzled?

"Huh?"

"You want me to finish, don't you?" as he looked at Chanel with bedroom eyes. She felt conflicted. She wanted to stop, but then she wanted to keep going.

"Okay," she responded. Chanel smiled; at the same time, she couldn't believe that she let him do that to her. Chanel, still in disbelief, stood and grabbed her robe off the ground. Afterward, she looked at her phone screen and fixed her hair. A habit of hers. I guess this was her way of looking presentable, even in moments of chaos. Chanel avoided eye contact with Trey, who was eyeing her. Like a snake, he seductively moved his way to behind Chanel and began to kiss her on the back of her neck. It sent shivers down her spine and woke her up. Just as he began to caress her body from behind, her cell phone rang. She looked down it was her aunt. Chanel pressed the mute button and let it ring. "Okay," Chanel said eagerly. "Let's go." She put her robe on and walked towards her front door. Her neighbor close behind. She stepped out into the hallway and closed the door behind her.

"Do you think I should lock it?"

"Sure, you can if you want." Chanel went back into her condo and grabbed her key. She came back into the hallway and locked the door. Both of them walked up the stairs together. Chanel was very silent. She didn't know how to respond. She still couldn't believe that she was going through with it. They arrived at his condo, and being a gentleman, he opened his door.

"After you, beautiful," he spoke with charm and delight. Chanel softly smiled and walked in. She started walking towards his couch.

"Nah, you can go into the bedroom baby," he said. Chanel just looked.

"Okay," she said. As she walked into his bedroom and sat on the bed. Trey shortly followed in and whispered.

"I can't wait to finish what I started," as he licked his lips. Chanel felt too nervous. She's never let an older man do what he's doing to her. It felt weird as she listened to Trey close and locked her door. She knew there was no turning back. When Trey walked into his bedroom, Trey got down on his hands and knees and crawled to Chanel. He crawled to her leg and started tugging at her robe.

Chanel began to undo the knot from her waist. Once she was fully exposed, he ordered her to prop her leg up on the bed. Chanel complied with his orders. He then lifted himself to lick her labia.

Chanel closed her eyes and tried not to think about what was happening to her. The faster, the better.

He then used his fingers to part her lips and traced his tongue to her clitoris. He massaged her clit with his tongue over and over and over again. Simultaneously, he started fingering her. In and out, his fingers went as he continued to suck on her clit. Chanel moaned out in ecstasy.

"You like that?" he asked between pauses.

"Mhmm," she replied

"Want me to keep going?"

"Yes," she replied. He stood up to meet her gaze. He rearranged the covers and laid her out on his bed. He pushed her thighs back with his hands and began to feast on her down below. Chanel arched her back and allowed this man to nibble, suck, and lick her most intimate parts.

"Cum for me," he said

"Huh?" Chanel asked. This woke her up.

"You heard me, cum. I want you to cum in my mouth". He said. Just then, Chanel kind of came back to reality. She all of a sudden, felt gross and exposed. But her body couldn't stop the feeling. She enjoyed the pleasure. Hated the conviction. Just as she began to have second thoughts, something told her to look down at Trey. Following her gut, she did, and Lord and behold, his face seemed strange. Extremely strange. The soft face of Trey looked sinister and devilish to her. He was watching her as he performed oral sex. His eyes were glued to her. Chanel began to feel uneasy.

"Cum for me," he said again. This time when he said it, Chanel was looking in his eyes. He frightened her. *Oh my God, what have I done?* But that wasn't it. His eyes began to flicker like a flame in the wind. His eyes, his face, his skin color, appeared to be different. His tongue was long and slender. The more Chanel studied his face; the more his appearance became demonic. At that realization, she suddenly became uninterested and turned off. Her vaginal dried up, and she was distant.

'Uhm," can you stop.

"Aww, come on baby, let me kiss it a little more," Trey pleaded, and he continued kissing her.

'Uhm, no. I'm sorry. Can you please stop?" Chanel asked again.

"Just one more kiss?" Trey said as he stopped. He looked Chanel in the face and said, "just one more kiss. I'm finishing up" then he proceeded to continue his "favor," Chanel felt sick. She wanted him to stop. She didn't feel comfortable anymore, and it was no longer doing it for her.

"Trey, please," Chanel said as she pushed his face away.

"Okay, okay," he said as he stood to his feet and leaned over to kiss her thighs. Chanel didn't want him kissing her at all. She felt dirty. She laid there as he finished licking and kissing her thighs. He tried to maneuver his way back down.

"Oh no," she responded as she bolted up.

"Hahaha, I wanted to see what you would do?" he said. Chanel placed a pretend smile on her face.

"I bet," she replied. Chanel stood up and walked in the living room, and sat down on his couch. Trey walked in behind her and sat down next to her. He leaned over and once again started kissing Chanel all over the back of her neck as he caressed her thigh. Chanel became annoyed. *I just want him to stop.* Chanel continued sitting on the couch, ignoring Trey. To her amazement, Trey tried to push Chanel over the arm of the sofa so that he can perform his "favor" on her, again.

"No," Chanel spoke strongly. This made Trey jump back. He eyed Chanel.

"What's wrong with you?" said in a firm voice.

"I'm just ready to go, and you keep going," she said in a playful tone. The truth is, she didn't want him to flip out on her again.

"Aw, ok," he started. "I'll stop," as he threw his hands in a defensive motion. Chanel was sensing the tension in the room. She hurriedly got up and walked towards his front door.

"Chanel," he called out from behind her.

"Yes," she answered as she turned around to face him. He opened his arms for a hug. Chanel winced.

"What, you don't trust me?" he groaned "didn't I tell you? I want you to be comfortable. That's my primary goal."

"I understand," she said. But Chanel didn't want to hug him. She didn't understand why he is so forceful. "I hope you have a good day," Chanel replied as she continued out of his front door. Trey was on her heels.

"So you not going to give me a hug?" he questioned. Chanel rolled her eyes and turned around for a second time to face him.

"Trey, why do I need to hug you? I mean, I said bye?"
"Don't be like that?"
"Be like what?"
"Acting all funny again. See, I knew I shouldn't never do that for you."
"What are you talking about?"
"See, all I'm trying to do is be your friend. And you're pushing me away. How you think that makes me feel?" he replied. Chanel couldn't believe how Trey was acting over a hug. *Like are you serious?*

"Trey, I think you're making this bigger than what it needs to be."

"Chanel, look, I like you. I think you are an amazing woman."

"Thank you," she replied.

"So why can't I give you a hug?" he questioned. Chanel was becoming more annoyed by the minute. Like why did she need to explain why she didn't want to hug him?

Chanel took a deep breath, "Well, because it seems like you don't know how to control yourself. Like when I say stop, you keep going, and I don't like that."

"Chanel, you know I will never hurt you," Trey started, "it pains me to know that you don't trust me."

"I mean," Chanel started,

"Nah, you don't trust me. And that makes me sad, because I haven't done anything to you," Trey finished. How did I become the bad guy here? Chanel looked Trey in his eyes saw the seriousness in his posture. This man is acting like the victim when he is the one who is responsible. Chanel didn't want to hug Trey, and here he is making her feel guilty. So Chanel huffed and caved to his demands,

"Okay, one hug," she replied and she put up one finger to show how serious she was, one hug. Trey made a face,

"C'mon, Chanel. You know I won't take advantage of you like that," Trey replied as he opened his arms. Chanel walked back over to Trey, who was more than ready to embrace her. Chanel reached her arms around him and tried to do a quick church hug. He didn't like it. He made a face.

"C'mon, Chanel, for real. I real a hug."

"That is a real hug," she replied. *What is it with this man?* Then Trey started to pout. Chanel puffed.

"Okay, one more hug," she said. She wrapped her arms around Trey who greeted her back with his warmth. The hug didn't start bad. It was a long embrace. Then suddenly, Trey began to caress Chanel and kissing on her neck as he pulled her close. Chanel delayed her response for a few seconds because she didn't know how to respond. Yes, it felt good, but she didn't want it. So she pulled back.

"No," she said. Trey puffed again,

"Chanel please."

"That's not a proper hug between two friends. That's more of a romantic hug," she said back in defense.

"Uh, ok, Chanel, whatever you say," Trey said with a sad look on his face.

"Okay, have a nice day Trey, I need to get some sleep for work tomorrow."

"Okay Chanel. Hopefully, you will spend the night with me, one day," he replied. Chanel quickly walked back into her condo and closed the door. She leaned back and took a deep breath. What the hell did I just do?

Road Blocks

Flashes back:

"So Chanel tell me why you're here? "

"Well, I need help."

"With what?"

"I don't know... I'm ashamed to say."

"Take your time, no judgment here."

"Well, I need help."

"With?"

"Well, I tried to kill myself, and I realize I need help."

"I see... What is going on in your life that made you feel like that?"

"It's a lot going on. I mean a lot, and I know I only have an hour."

"It's okay; we can schedule for another day if need to. Don't focus on time. I am here to help you."

"Okay,"... Chanel took a breath. "I was raped by my ex-boyfriend." Chanel took another breath. She began to cry. "It was one of the most traumatic experiences of my life. I didn't feel I had the right to say I was raped because I felt like I let him do it."

"Well, tell me exactly what happened."

"Well, we were messing around in my dorm room, which is normal. Sometimes we would do oral sex on each other, sometimes we would get naked, and I would rub on him, we would kiss, all of that." Chanel looked at the psychiatrist whose face was too hard to read. "So this particular time, he kept putting the head of his penis at the opening of my vagina, and it felt like he was trying to stick it in. I kept telling him that I didn't want to have sex. That I didn't like that he was putting the head of his penis there. So he got argumentive with me and told me to relax. He's not going to do anything to me. He just likes sticking his head right there because it feels good, and I need to trust him. So we continued kissing and playing around, and like before, he stuck his head near the opening of my vagina. I didn't say anything because I was trying to trust him. Plus, like 5 seconds before, he said he was not going to do anything to me. To trust him. So I didn't say anything. And it just happened. He just stuck his penis inside me. I didn't say anything. I just laid there. I didn't know what to say or do. I was hurt that he was doing that to me. I was also afraid of what he could do to me. So I didn't say anything, I just laid there. I don't remember all of it. I just remember that when he stopped, I just laid there. I didn't say anything. And there was blood all over my covers. He didn't seem concerned about what he just did. He was happy because in his mind he felt that we had sex." Chanel looked down at the floor. This was the first time she's told this story, and she felt guilty. She felt that what happened to her was her fault.

"Well, that's rape, honey. It doesn't matter how you said no; the fact is that you said no, and he did it anyway."

"Well, I don't feel like it. I feel like it's my fault. I feel like I let him do it."

"What makes you say that?"

"Because I froze. I didn't do anything."

"What would you say if I told you that your response is normal?"

"What is normal?"

"You freezing. That's a normal response. Are you familiar with fight and flight?"

"Yes."

"Well, did you know there is another response that is not talked about as much?"

"No."

"It's called the freeze response. Sometimes in danger, the brain tells the body to freeze because it feels that the stimulus you are experiencing is too dangerous to fight back. Freezing is the body's way of protecting itself. You do not have control over this response. It's automatic. It's located in the hypothalamus part of your brain. So, when you froze during your rape, it was your body's way of protecting you. You did nothing wrong. You were innocent." Chanel studied her psychiatrist face. She cried some more. She couldn't believe what the psychiatrist was saying.

"Can I have more tissues, please?"

"Of course, that's what they are there for." Chanel grabbed more tissues. She let the words of her therapist sink that the rape wasn't her fault.

"It's just hard for me to accept that. He made me feel guilty about it. He said that I should have known sex was coming. It's hard for me to move on from this because I'm still hurting."

"That's understandable. Did you report your rape?"

"No, ma'am... I didn't think anyone would believe me. I felt like I should have fought back harder. But I didn't. I just laid there. I let him do that to me. Well, at least in my mind."

"I see." Chanel closed her eyes.

"Ever since this rape, I don't find myself being as confident as I use to be anymore. I'm afraid to date. I'm afraid to speak up. As of lately, I feel as if I give in to what other people want, and I don't stick up for myself. It's hard. I find myself doing things that I don't want to do deep down inside."

"So you're letting people take advantage of you?"

"Yes."

"That's a typical response for rape victims to lose confidence after being raped. Some rape victims see it as if their power was taken away. However, you have to take power back."

"I don't know if I can?"

"What makes you believe that?"

"Because I just don't see it happening for me."

"Chanel, can I ask you a question?"

"Yes?"

"Do you value yourself?" Chanel looked at her therapist in the eyes. She couldn't answer the question. Everything that she's been through. Everything that she's experienced. All the pain, the trauma, the hurt. She realized many lot of situations she found herself in after the rape directly correlated to how she felt about herself. Chanel guilted herself. She found herself dirty. She treated herself meanly. She didn't believe she desired mercy. She just stared her therapist in the eyes and began to cry.

It's been a few days since Chanel last let Trey perform oral sex on her. She would think about him now and then, how he felt, and how he talked too. It was weird. Part of her wanted him, and part of her didn't. Part of her wanted to continue, and part of her wanted to get far away from him. Then another part of her felt guilty. A pang of deep guilt. She felt as if she was letting this man take advantage of her. She didn't like the way that the guilt tripped her. She didn't like the way that he made her feel guilty if she would say no. She felt like he was trying to take control of her. She just wanted peace of mind.

Chanel laid out on her bed and stared at the ceiling. While she was lying on her bed, her phone beeped. It was Courtney. Chanel didn't tell her friend what happened that night. She knew Courtney would be pissed. So she opted not to say anything at all. She picked up her phone and began texting.

"Hey girl," Courtney texted.

"Hey," Chanel said back.

"What's up with you? I haven't spoken to you in a few days. I had messaged you back. Just wanting to make sure everything is okay."

"Aww, thanks, girl. I appreciate that. I've been doing fine. You know, same ole, same ole."

"Okay. That sounds good."

"Anything new or exciting? How are you and that neighbor of yours?" Chanel shifted uncomfortably on her bed. She didn't like the idea of lying to her friend; however, she didn't want her friend to worry.

"Girl, things are cool. Trey is a pretty cool person. I've learned so much from him. I don't have any complaints."

"Aw, okay. Are you guys dating or just friends?"

"We're just friends, nothing serious."

"Well, that's good because you know he's way too old for you to be in a relationship with him."

"I feel you." *I better not tell her that I let him perform oral sex on me.* Chanel knew that if Courtney knew the truth, that would be the end of it.

"Yea, so when are you going to let me come over there? I can't wait to see the new place."

"Yes, girl, I can't wait for you to come to visit. Just let me know when and I'll do my best to be here."

"Okay, sounds good. Maybe sometime this weekend."

"Okay, sounds good."

"Ohh, I can't wait! I'm so excited."

"Me too." Just as Chanel finished texting Courtney, Chanel heard a knock at the door. She pushed herself off the bed and walked towards her front door. She peeped through the hole and saw that it was Trey. *Oooh, I wonder what he wants.* Chanel found herself instantly excited at the sight of Trey. She fixed her clothes, brushed her hair out of the way, and opened the door.

"Hey Trey," she responded with excitement in her voice.

"Hey, wassup," he responded, "how are you?"

"I'm doing good. Yourself?"

"I'm doing good. I know what can make me better."

"Oh, what's that?" Chanel asked, confused. Trey didn't say anything. He let his eyes do the talking. He looked Chanel up and down. He took her pointer and middle finger and brought them to his mouth as he spilled them into a V. He took his tongue and flicked his tongue in-between as if he was performing oral sex. Chanel felt disgusted. Eww, she thought to herself. Trying to play if off,

"Oh, is that how you feel?" unamused.

"Yea," he said with a rolling laugh. Chanel was disgusted with herself. *Why on earth did I let that man perform oral sex on me? Why?*

"I just wanted to stop by and see how things were going with you?"

"Things are okay. Same ole, same ole. Nothing special."

"Oh, okay. Were you okay with me doing that to you?"

"Well, it kind of caught me by surprise. I wasn't expecting that, honestly."

"I didn't take you too fast, did I?"

"I kind of felt like you did. I kind of felt like I just gave you what you wanted." Trey made a face at that comment.

"Chanel, you know I wouldn't do anything to hurt you. I just want you comfortable."

"I understand, I truly do."

"Are you sure?" Trey asked.

"Positive," she replied. "Speaking of that, I think I won't let you do that anymore. It was nice, but I don't want to create a of habit of that, especially if we're supposed to be friends." Trey made another face.

"Chanel, where is all this coming from?"

"What you mean?"

"It just seems like you are upset with me, and now you want to distance yourself."

"I didn't say that. All I'm saying is that I just don't want to do that anymore. It did feel terrific, don't get me wrong" Chanel doubled back because she knew Trey would twist her words. She didn't want him to become upset. "I just think for us to have a good friendship, we shouldn't do things like that."

"You're right," he said. "I respect that."

"Thank you."

"Okay, well, I won't take any more of your time."

"Okay, see you around." Chanel waved as she closed her door. Chanel turned around and walked back to her bedroom. *Well, that was easier than I thought.* Just as she was beginning to sit down on her bed, she heard another knock on her door. She went to investigate.

"Who is it?" she called out.

"It's me," Trey said. *Oh, God, what does he want?* Chanel opened the door for a second time.

"Yes, Trey?" she answered.

"Hey, I just wanted to make sure that everything was cool between us."

"Yea, it is. What makes you ask that?"

"Nothing, in particular, I just wanted to make sure that everything was cool between us. I just want to make sure you are comfortable."

"I'm fine, Trey. I appreciate you for doing that." Trey made a face.

"What's wrong?"

"It's nothing. Okay, I won't bother you again."

"Okay. See you later," Chanel waved bye with a smile. She closed her door again. She walked into the kitchen to pour herself a glass of cold water. Before she could even reach up and grab her cup out of the cupboard, another knock was at her door. Chanel started to become annoyed. She knew it was Trey.

"Who is it?" she asked.

"It's me, Trey," he replied.

"Okay, one second please," Chanel replied. She grabbed her cup and poured herself some water. She stood near her counter as she guzzled the water down. She then proceeded to walking back to her front door and opening it.

"Yes," she said, trying to have a polite smile.

"One more thing," he started, "I hate when you do that?"

"Do what?"

"That, hey... with that fake smile. I don't like it. It's so fake."

"Oh," Chanel replied with disdain. "That was rude."

"How so?"

"Because where do you get off telling me that my smile bothers you? I was trying to be polite."

"Oh, that's you being polite. My bad. Well you should change that. It doesn't come off as genuine." Chanel rolled her eyes at him. He was starting to annoy her like he always does.

"Is that what you wanted?" she asked.

"No, I wanted something else."

"Oh, and that is?"

"I just wanted to say, Chanel, I don't want to make you uncomfortable. I enjoyed doing that for you, and I wouldn't mind doing that for you again. I'm sorry that it has to end."

"I mean, I do appreciate that, but I just don't know if it's the right thing to do in our friendship. That's why I was so hesitant to say whether or not I wanted to spend the night at your house. I originally told you to know. But then you started pressing me and making me feel bad. So I felt like I had to choose. As you can see, I still haven't spent the night at your house."

"I see that, and I picked up on that. Remember, I'm not trying to pressure you. I truly enjoy you. You are just so damn beautiful, and I like being around you." Trey plead.

"I understand," Chanel replied. She didn't. She didn't like him making her feel like she had to give in to him because he liked doing something.

"I'm sorry this is hard for you to comprehend," Chanel replied, trying to be sympathetic.

"Do you?" Trey said.

"Yea, I understand."

"Well, thank you for understanding," he replied, "Can I have a hug?" Trey asked as he opened his arms.

"No," Chanel said.

"C'mon Chanel, why not?"

"Because your hugs always go overboard."

"Chanel, I promise I won't go overboard. I promise. Just trust me." He said.

"No, Trey, I don't want to hug you."

"Okay," he said with a face.

"Have a nice day Trey" Chanel said as she went to close her door. Trey put his foot in the way to prevent it from closing. Chanel immediately looked up. Trey embraced Chanel anyway, just holding her in his arms. Chanel felt violated. *Like why is this man hugging me after I told him no?* Chanel didn't hug him back. She started ruminating at her hugging him. She was pissed. Trey whispers, "so you no going to hug me back?"

"I just told you that I didn't want to hug."

"It's just one hug Chanel, what is that going to hurt." Feeling defeated, Chanel gives in and gave him embraced him back.

"See, that wasn't so bad," he responded. The two swayed in the hallway for some time, embracing each other. Trey clung closely to Chanel's small body. His big overpowering arms swallowed her up. Chanel noticed his body heat. He always felt so warm. His embrace was soft. She did like how he feels; however, she always knew that he will go overboard. Just as she predicted, he went overboard again. His hands started to rub down her back. Chanel was paying attention to the placement of his hands. Soon his hands began to caress her entire back from her shoulder to the beginning of her waist. Chanel stiffened. Then suddenly, he kissed her on the neck. Chanel immediately backed away.

"See, see what you do," she replied.

"I'm sorry, I didn't mean to go overboard. It just that your body is so comfortable."

"I bet. I'm going in the house now."

"Okay. Have a nice day," trey said as he moved out of Chanel's doorway. Chanel closed the door. Trey's body felt so good, and she felt herself get excited. However, she did not want to go down that path again. *Let me go freshen up.* She walked into her bathroom and grabbed a towel. She washed around her neck and under her boobs. The heat made her sweat just a little bit. Chanel then went and laid on her bed. She looked down at her phone and thought about her classmate.

"Hey girl," as she sent a text message to her classmate.

"Wassup. How are things going?"

"Things are going good. I have a question I wanted to ask you?"

"What's that?'

"Remember that neighbor I was telling you about?"

"Yea, the one that wanted you to spend the night. How did they end up for you?"

"Well, I didn't spend the night with him."

"Well, that's good," her classmate replied.

"Yea, but not. I'm in a bigger problem."

"What's that?"

"I let him perform oral sex on me?"

"oh word, how was it?'

"It was good; it felt nice. He's a freak."

"I bet, older men typically are. So what's the problem?"

"Do you think it's a bad thing that I let him eat me out?"

"Nah, that's not too bad. Just as long as it stays like that, don't let him have sex with you. If he wants coochie, then he must pay a bill or something. Ain't nothing free."

"Really?"

"Yea girl, that's what my momma says."

"Oh, I never heard that before."

"Yea, that's kind of old school." Her classmate responded.

"Oh, okay. I thought it was a bad thing that I let him do it."

"I mean, if you don't want it, you don't have to. It's up to you."

"Right. It is," Chanel responded. Chanel laid back in her bed and looked at the ceiling. She looked down at her watch. She had just enough time to get a decent nap in before going to the library to study.

Flashes back
"So Chanel, tell me about your father."

"What about him?" she responded.

"What was your relationship like with him?"

"I didn't have a relationship with him. I barely saw him. He was in and out of my life a lot. He died from a drug overdose."

"What was your interactions like when he was around?"

'Well, we would talk. He would ask me about what I was doing at the time. You know the school, grades, boys, etc."

The therapist was very quiet after Chanel answered the question. She just jotted down a few notes on her notepad. Chanel watched with intensity as the psychiatrist continued to write away. Then she finally asked Chanel a question.

"How did your dad treat your mother?" Chanel made a face. "To be honest, I don't remember."

"Okay, can you think back for me as best as you can?"

"Yes," Chanel answered. Chanel was silent. She started to trace her mind to her childhood. Looking for anything that could be the answer for what her psychiatrist is looking for. She thought long and hard then finally,

"He was distant," She answered.

"What do you mean by distant?"

"I can't explain," Chanel answered. The psychiatrist gave her a small smile. "It's okay, take your time." Chanel was confused about the activity, and asked, "What exactly am I supposed to be looking for?"

"Well, I want you to think back as best as you can too how your parents interacted with each other? How did your father treat your mother if you can remember." Chanel huffed.

"Okay, let me think a little harder." Chanel closed her eyes and begun to think harder about her mother and father. She could remember things like they seemed happy. They slept in the same bed. They seemed like a happy family. Then one day, they weren't together anymore. Her mother would become frustrated with her dad. He would always blame her mother for everything.

'They would have disagreements sometimes," Chanel started.

"Okay, about?"

"Me."

"What exactly about you?"

"Things he blamed her for."

"What kind of things?"

"Things like, not being around. Or why they weren't together. He would blame her. A lot."

"Mhm…" the psychiatrist nodded and jotted down more notes.

"Okay, how did that make you feel?" she asked Chanel.

"I was upset."

"About?"

"Them not being together. Them fighting. It would bother me a lot. I was furious, and sometimes, I blamed her too."

"Mhm…" her psychiatrist nodded. "How did your father show up for you?"

"What do you mean?"

"I mean, how did he treat you? Was he consistent? Was he fair?" How did he show up?"

"Well, he wasn't always consistent. Sometimes I would see him, and sometimes I wouldn't."

"And when he wouldn't show up, how did that make you feel?"

"It made me feel that I didn't matter."

"How did you react to him, not showing up and being consistent?"

"I would be despondent and wonder why. I thought if I changed something, or if my mother would stop being mean, then maybe our life would go back to normal."

"Okay. We are getting somewhere. How did your father explain, not showing up to you?"

"What you mean?'

"I mean, on the days where he didn't show up and be consistent, what would he say in his defense."

"He would always tell me that he was sorry. That he had things going on. That he's trying. That he loves me very much, and I should know that when things get better, he will take care of me better." Chanel said as tears began to roll down her face.

"Did things ever get better?"

"No," Chanel put her head down and wept. "He kept doing the same thing over and over and over again."

"And what did you do?" Or better yet, how did you respond?"

"I kept believing him over and over and over again. Because I believed that one day, he would change."

Chanel wakes up out of her sleep. The sun is starting to set.

"Shoot, I over slept," she moaned as she rolled out of bed. "I suppose I can get a little studying down." So she still gathered up her things for a late-night study session in the library.

She headed into the bathroom to freshen up. She used the restroom, brushed her teeth, fixed her hair, wiped her face, and cleaned the eye boogers from the corners of her eyes. Chanel looked herself over in the mirror. She admired her beautiful dark skin. Her lovely 4c hair. Her beautiful high cheekbones. She was stunning. She headed back to her bedroom and retrieved her phone. Near the door sat her bookbag. She did a quick five minute check to make sure she had everything. "Keys, cell phone, book bag, watch, and wallet. All set" She opened her door and stepped into the hallway. As she locked her door, her neighbor was coming down the steps.

"I thought I heard you," he said with a cheerful grin.

"Uhm, yea," she said. She wasn't all that happy to see him."

"So, where are you off to?" he asked.

"Why?" she questioned.

"I was just curious," he responded, throwing his hands up.

"Oh," Chanel responded. She finished locking her door and proceeded out the main entrance without answering his question.

"So you're not going to tell me?" he asked.

"Uhm, do I have to?"

"Nah, you don't."

"Lol, okay. Well, have a good evening."

"You too, Ms. Lady. Hopefully, I see you tonight." Chanel looked back at him. His gaze was lowered, and she already knew what that meant. She quickly walked outside and headed to her car. She chirped the lock and performed her usual care routine. When everything was adjusted, she turned the key in the ignition and was on her way. "Maybe some music will help." She turned the radio on and blared an upbeat alternative song. It took her no time to arrive at school and find a parking spot near the ground level. She parked her car and gathered her things. She walked into the library and found a seat on the ground level. She pulled out her laptop, notebook, textbook, pens, highlighters, pencils, and pens. She opened her textbook and started reading the assigned text. However, she was distracted. Her thought's kept going back to Trey. She wanted to feel Trey's tongue on her clitoris, and she was embarrassed to admit it. *"C'mon, girl. Focus on the task at hand. Focus!"* she urged herself. She opened her notebook and read her notes. She made it to page five before she started thinking of Trey again. *"Okay, maybe I should get up and walk around."* So Chanel got up cruised the library. She has walked the first floor, looking at all the resource books. She then took the steps to the second floor and walked in between the aisles. She then went into the library's basement and found a cool couch next to a statue, and sat there for a while. She tried to relax and take her mind off Trey. He was entertaining, but she knew that she should not be messing around with that older man. She knew he was no good for her. She knew he all about him. She stood up and walked back upstairs to the main floor of the library. She found her table and sat down. She opened her textbook and matched her notebook to a clean page. She grabbed her pen and attempted to write her notes. Unfortunately, the desire she had for Trey was too great, and she gave in to her wants. So she packed up her books, her belongings and proceeded to her car. She got in and threw everything into the passenger seat. She turned her key in the ignition and drove home. She distanced herself from the idea that she was doing something wrong. She tried not to think about what she was about to go home and do. She pulled into her usual parking spot and grabbed her things. She chirped her car door and walked into her condo building. Chanel stood in front of her condo door and unlocked the door. She quickly sat her bag down and headed to the bathroom. She grabbed a towel and ran some warm water. She grabbed her bar of dove soap and lightly made her towel soapy. She cleaned herself before heading upstairs. She patted herself dry and adjusted her clothes. She walked back out her condo door and proceeded upstairs to Trey's condo. Without even thinking, she knocked on his door. "Who is it?" she heard him call out. 'It's me, Chanel," she responded. He opened his door. He had on a white t-shirt, black pajama pants, and house shoes.

He had a durag on his head to protect his braids.
"Yes, Ms. Lady," he said.

"I Just wanted to let you know that I was back," she said. She didn't want him to pick up on the fact she was there for him to perform oral sex on her.

"Well, thank you for telling me," he said. "Where did you go? You weren't there long?"

"I went to the library, but I couldn't study, so I called it a night."

'Oh, okay. Well, at least you tried. School can be hard."

"Yea, it can be a time."

"Hold on for a second," he said as he stepped back into his condo. Chanel took a seat on the next level of steps and waited for Trey to come back out. When he finally reemerged, he closed the door behind him. He took a seat on the upper rear of the lower level.

'So, what's on your mind?" he asked.

"Nothing. Just bored. I'm a little tired.""oh, long day, huh?"

"Yea, it kind of was. A very long day. I slept the majority of it."

"Oh, yea."

"Yea."

"Hey Chanel, I want to ask you a question?"

"Yes?" "Is there a real reason why you don't trust me?" "What you mean? She asked.

"I mean you act scared of me. Like I'm going to do something to you."

"Oh," Chanel responded. She looked down. She didn't know how to answer his question. She didn't understand what he was hinting at. "I'm not sure what you mean."

"Don't worry about it. Just know I want to make sure you are comfortable in everything I do. I care about you.

I enjoy our friendship, and I can't wait for the day you let me make you mines, officially. Chanel rolled her eyes at the thought. She knew there was no future for them. But at this moment, she wanted him.

Trey reached out and started caressing Chanel's leg. Chanel felt herself become moist just by his touch. "Chanel, I would do that for you," he said.

"Do what?" she responded.

"You know what I'm talking about. You taste so good," he responded. Chanel laughed. "Boy, you crazy if you think I would let you do that to me out here in this hallway," she chuckled. To her surprise Trey got on his knees and came to Chanel. He started kissing her lower legs. Chanel felt herself become wetter. Trey took his time kissing her legs as he made his way up to her thighs. Chanel, who had on shorts, became worried. Trey lifted his head and said, "take your shorts off."

'Are you sure?" she asked.

"Yes, nobody is coming at this hour." So Chanel listened to Trey and took her shorts off. Trey spread her thighs and began to the nipple on her through her panties. Chanel moaned in ecstasy. The sensation of him kissing her through the fabric was a nice touch. Then he ordered Chanel to stand up. So she followed. He then took Chanel's spot and told her to lower herself onto his face. She complied. He then; moved her panties to the side and started eating her out on the hallway's steps. She leaned her head back and rolled her eyes close. His warm tongue felt so good to her throbbing clit. He started chewing softly on her labia. He slowly inserted his finger into her hot and wet vagina. Chanel began to rock her hips and grind her vagina onto his face. Trey reached up and guided her hips back and forth, and he continued to feast on her lady parts. Chanel then began to hump Trey's face.

Trey lifted his head and I asked, "do you like it?"

"Yes," she responded.

"I can tell. You're very wet. You should come to my apartment."

"For?'

"You'll see." Having no other choice, Chanel agreed to go into Trey's apartment. She gathered her shorts and walked in with extremely exposed. Trey led Chanel to his bedroom. The lights were already off. He laid Chanel down on the bed. She heard her rummaging around on his dresser. She couldn't make out exactly what he was doing. When he finally came back he kneeled between Chanel's legs.

"Would you be interested in butt play?"

"Huh?"

"Have you ever had someone play with your butt before?"

"No," Chanel answered.

"Well, are you interested?" he asked.

"Sure," she said.

"Okay, relax," he said. So Trey, with the butt plug already in his hand with a condom on it inserted the plug into Chanel's butt. She winced. The sensation was new. Trey slowly worked the butt plug in, and out and he continued to eat Chanel's throbbing vagina. Chanel moaned and moaned as Trey continued to take her to her limit.

"You like that baby?' he asked.

"Yes," Chanel moaned out in ecstasy.

"How would you feel if I f*** in your ass?" Trey asked. At this point, Chanel was too dizzy from ecstasy to even pay attention to what he was asking her.

"Sure," she said, without even thinking.

"Okay," Trey said. He disappeared for a second and came back with a second condom. He placed the condom on his manhood. He added a fair amount of lube on his penis and told Chanel to get on her hands and knees. Chanel listened. She turned over and positioned herself. Trey slowly worked himself inside Chanel anus. He was very gentle as he entered her. Chanel never felt this before. The pressure of his d*** in her butt was a new sensation. She moaned even louder at the pleasure and slight pain she received from Trey. He f***** her gently from behind. Chanel loved every minute of it. She sighed, and Trey joined her in her moaning.

"Oh, Chanel baby, you feel so good. I wanna feel your p****," he said.

"Um, no," she responded. That's when she came back to reality. "Okay, that's fair," he said. However, at this point, Chanel realized how deep she was. Not only did she allow this man to perform oral sex on her again, but she also allowed him to perform anal sex. As she looked through the blinds in Trey's bedroom window, she wondered, *"Will I ever be free?"*

Entangled

"Mhmm, yes, ah, yes Trey," Chanel moaned. Trey, who was feasting on her p**** from the back on his couch. This has become her new norm. Since the first day he ate her out, she's been addicted. From sun up to sundown, Chanel had her legs wide open any time of day, allowing Trey to carve new valleys and streams into her with his tongue. "You like that baby?" he asked.

"Yes," she moaned.

"You wanna ride my face?"

"Yes!" Trey got up and sat on the couch, and Chanel stood and positioned herself over him. She lowered herself on top of his face. She moved, rotated, and rocked her hips back and forth. She rolled her eyes to the back of her head and let her stream of juices moisten his face and mustache.

"Feed me your p****," Trey commanded. Chanel squatted up and down, pushing Trey's face deeper inside her. She leaned her face against the cool wall. Trey thrusted his tongue inside her. He stuck one finger in her butt. Chanel reached down and caressed Trey manhood.

"Let me stick it in your butt?" he asked. Chanel thought about it. This has been a new experience for her. The first time Trey did anal sex on Chanel, it was a new sensation however, since she's been coming over here day and night, that's become the new thing.

"Okay," she replied. Chanel stood up, and Trey got up off the couch.

"Bend over," he said to her. Chanel bent over the arm of the couch. Trey spits on his p**** and Chanel butt hole. He slowly worked his way inside her. Chanel moaned in ecstasy as Trey started doing her in her butt. Chanel felt every inch of his manhood. Her vagina throbbed below.

"Play with your p****," he moaned. That was another thing Chanel had to get used to. His way of sex. She found him to be somewhat perverted. It was different. When she did have sex with guys, it was different. They did basic stuff. Trey's idea of sex was very kinky. He liked butt plugs, vibrators, toys, anal sex, etc. This was stuff that he owned already, which did send alarms off in Chanel's minds at the time. She couldn't understand why a man would own all this stuff. He claimed it came from his previous relationship with the woman from his past. Which was all fine and all; however, she still couldn't understand why he still had it. Chanel complied. She started to rub her clitoris as Trey f**** from behind. Trey was a monster to her sometimes. She couldn't explain it. She couldn't explain why she felt that way. Nor could she explain why she continued to come over here time and time again, knowing that he was no good for her, he was sexually perverted, and he was oftentimes manipulative and narcissistic.

"Chanel baby, I wanna stick it in your p**** so bad." He moaned. Chanel didn't respond. He's been begging for vaginal intercourse since the first time he performed oral sex on her. That was the one thing she wouldn't let him do. She already felt dirty, allowing him to do all these things to her :she couldn't live with herself if she let him stick it in there. That was her saving grace. The most she will let him do is let him f*** with a vibrating pink dildo or his fingers.

"You already know the rules, no vaginal sex."

"I know, baby. I just wanted to ask." Chanel rolled her eyes. It was moments like this where she regretted letting him do it the first time. She regretted being her. She regretted saying yes.

"Turnover," he said. Chanel followed. He laid her on her back and started eating her out again. He pushed her legs back and exposed her clitoris. He sucked on it lovingly. That sent a shift into Chanel spine. The sensation of him kissing, licking, and sucking on her clit brought her on the brink of coming. Chanel's thighs started to twitch. Trey knew what that meant. He stopped abruptly and picked up the vibrating pink dildo on his table. He turned the speed on high and placed it directly on her clitoris. Chanel moaned louder. Trey watched with pure enjoyment. He started to jerk himself off at the site of Chanel climaxing.

"I wanna come with you baby," he moaned. He jerked himself off harder and helped the toy on Chanel's clit.

"YES!" she moaned louder and louder.

"Baby, please let me stick it in. Please," Trey begged. Chanel shook her head, no! She refused to let this man stick his penis in her. Luckily, she didn't have to worry about that. She came, and so did he a few moments later. Chanel laid on the couch, fully naked in awe and disgust. She loved the pleasure, hated herself. Trey, on the other hand, loved every minute of it.

"Damn baby, that felt so good. I love watching you cum," he said as he caressed her naked body. Chanel felt sick. She was ready to go. She sat up. "yea, it's always nice watching you too", she lied. She hated looking at him. She thought he was a demon. Chanel stood up and started putting on her clothes. Trey stood behind her and started kissing the back of her neck. She threw up on her mouth.

"Chanel, I don't want you to leave," he said. Chanel looked at the time. It was 6:00 in the morning, and she needed to start getting ready for work. She barely slept during the night. She tossed and turned and thought about Trey. Then the time she could have been using for rest, she was over her with him.

"I have to work."

"I know, maybe you will consider spending the night with me. Since that's what I originally wanted."

"Maybe," she replied. She finished putting on all her clothes as Trey tucked his penis back into his pants. She walked to the front door, and Trey walked closely behind her. As she reached for the door, Trey came out and put his hand on the door as a way to keep it closed.

"Call off," he asked.

"Uhm, no" she responded.

"Lol, I'm just kidding," he said. Chanel, still facing the door, rolled her eyes. She was ready to go. She didn't want to be her. She only came to get her p***** ate. That's it! She huffed. Trey wrapped his arms around her.

"I just like holding you like this. It feels so good. You feel so good. You taste so good. I wish we can stay like this forever." Chanel gagged. She knew he was serious, and if she doesn't get up out of this house, he will try to make his way down to eat her out again.

"Thank you, Trey. I appreciate being over here with you too. But I have to go."

"I know. I'll let you free," he said. He opened his arms and opened the door for Chanel. Chanel stepped into the hallway with a sign of relief. Chanel walked towards the steps. She turned around to see Trey standing in his doorway with bedroom eyes.

"Bye, Trey" she said as she walked down the steps.

"Bye Chanel, see you later if you will let me," he replied. Chanel continued to walk down the steps and back into her condo. It was 6:15, and she was nowhere near ready for work. She had to hurry up and get cleaned up so she can make it there by 7:00 am.

She took a quick shower, fixed her hair, makeup, and put on her clothes. She grabbed her purse and rushed out the door. She hopped in the car and headed towards her job. On the highway, she drove 20 mph over the speed limit. She was trying her best to maneuver during morning rush traffic. She finally arrived at 6:56 am. She had just enough time she runs towards the time clock. Her friend Bebe said,

"Girl, you better hurry up."

"I'm trying," Chanel said. Chanel got to the time clock and realized she left her work badge at home.

"Oh, crap," she responded.

"What's wrong?" Bebe asked.

"I left my badge at home."

"Oh well, just fill out a timesheet card. Don't worry about it."

"You right."

"Yea, why are you so late this morning anyway. That's not like you."

"Rough morning," Chanel said, "I overslept." She lied. She didn't want Bebe to know the real reason why she was late. Bebe looked Chanel over. Chanel is looking confused.

"What?"

"Oh, nothing." Chanel shrugged it off and walked to her desk. Bebe sat down beside Chanel, still looking her over.

"Why do you keep staring at me. Is it something on my face?" Chanel asked.

"No," Bebe started, "but there is something in your neck." Chanel grabbed her cellphone and turned the camera on. Chanel saw that there was a small passion mark on her neck. *Oh crap,* she thought to herself. Trey must have put that there.

"So, are you going to tell me what happened?" Bebe said.

"Uhm, I don't want to?" Chanel started. She was ashamed to tell Bebe the truth.

"mh, Okay, Chanel." Bebe turned around and logged into her computer. Chanel looked at her computer screen with a blank expression. She couldn't believe she had a passion mark on her neck, and left her badge at home.

What was she thinking going over there this morning? Chanel huffed.

"I have a confession."

"What's that?"

"I've been seeing this guy?"

"I can see that?" Bebe laughed. "Who is he?"

"He's my neighbor?"

"Oh Lord hasn't anyone ever told you not to mess around with your neighbors. They bring nothing but trouble! Nothing but trouble!"

"Yea, well, that's who I have been seeing. We're not in a relationship or anything, though."

"Oh, okay, how old is he?"

"35."

"Chanel, he's 35?"

"How old are you?"

"19"

"Chanel, you are a baby compared to that man. What were you thinking?"

"I mean…I just… I don't know."

"How did all this get started?"

"He saw me in the hallway on the first day I moved in. I ignored him. He's very handsome. He was smiling at me, and I mugged him back. I just walked to my car."

"Okay, and?"

"That was it."

"No, Chanel, how did it lead up to you getting a hickey on your neck."

"Well, like over for the next few days, I would see him in the hallway a lot. I would still pay him no mind. He would try to start up small talk, and I would be very short with him. One day, he told me that I was very unapproachable and that he thought I was cute. That threw me off. Then he proceeded to tell me that he would like to start a friendship with me. I started feeling bad that I treated him so meanly. So I started being nicer to him and started speaking to him. You are having a small conversation here and there. Then one day, he invited me over to his place for seafood. I love seafood. We were just chilling and having lots of fun. He seemed like a cool dude. We got a lot closer that day. So we just continued talking to each other. Going to each other houses. Then it was one day, my aunt brought some food over to my house. I had way too much to eat and shared it with him. I just wanting to show gratitude and appreciate him sharing his food with me. I can't remember if it was that day or another day that he asked me would I be interested in spending the night at his house."

"He asked you to spend the night at his house?"

"Yes."

"He sounds desperate, Chanel."

"Oh."

"Is there more?"

"Yes."

"Oh, Lord."

"So I declined to spend the night at his house. He understood, so he says. But then, he began to pressure me a lot about staying over at his place. I also forgot to mention, he pushed up on me one of the days I was visiting him. That pissed me off. I didn't speak to him for a few days. He would knock on my door constantly, and I ignored him. I didn't feel like explaining myself to him. Especially, since I've already showed signs of not liking that type of thing. Oh, I also forgot to mention it was one particular time I did open the door and he started getting all loud with me and telling me that I was mean and selfish. I should have opened my door when he was knocking on it those past few days that I was making a big deal out of him asking me to spend the night at his house. I was so confused. I left, and went to school. So while I'm at school, I look up and see him there standing on the second floor of the student center."

"Wait, he followed you to school?

"Yes!"

"Oh my God, Chanel."

"What did you do?"

"I was freaked out that he followed me to school. When I saw him, I choked on my water. My classmate that I was hanging out with that day was concerned about me. I guess I started acting weird. Anyway, I couldn't focus on my work anymore. Soo, I got up and proceeded to head home. When I got to the elevator, he was standing there."

"Oh my. This sounds like a movie girl. He's crazy."

"So on the elevator, he apologized to me for his behavior. But I told him that it wasn't okay that he follows me. Especially follow me to school. Are you crazy? He told me that he's sorry and that he didn't mean to do that to me. That he cares about me and just wants to be my friend. He also confessed that he likes me a lot and would like to get to know me deeper. He wants to make me *his*, as he says. I wasn't all that sold. I don't remember everything that happened in the elevator. I just remember he kissed me very gently. His lips felt like pillows. After our kiss, he went home. I was able to function after that. I went to the library and got my work done. So anyway, we had another disagreement about something. I can't remember what about. But, he came over to my house when he did. I had just come out of the shower. I had my bathrobe on. We discussed what the problem was and then before you know it, he was kissing me again. I can't remember what lead up to it. I felt a bit weird with him hugging and kissing on me with my bathrobe. He placed his hands underneath my robe and realized I was naked. That excited him, and me too a little bit, then he then leads me to my bedroom and ate me out on my bed."

"Girl, what?" Yes, he ate me out on my bed. Then I followed him back to his place, and he ate me out again. I know I shouldn't have gone. But his tongue felt so good. It was euphoric. So anyway, that's kind of how all this got started. I think a few days or weeks went by before he ate me out again. But leading up to that, he would constantly ask me if I would allow him to hug me. I would say no because he's kind of weird to me."

"What you mean, weird?'

"Well, when he hugs me, he always wants to go further than the hug, which is what I don't like. I just want peace. But he wants to keep going. He likes to feel all over my body, kiss me on the neck, touch, etc. It's just too much. When I protest that I don't want to hug him, he gets mad at me and makes me feel bad saying that he's not going to do anything to me. That I can trust him, and he just wants me to be comfortable. I don't like that. Because sometimes I feel like he's guilting me into hugging him. I even try to give him church hugs, and he's not satisfied with that. Then it was one day; I was extremely horny. I mean extremely horny. I couldn't focus on nothing. I went over to his condo with the intent of getting eaten out. We talked in the hallway for a little bit before he started kissing my legs and thighs. Then boom, he ate me out on the steps."

"Oh my God, Chanel. You letting this older man do that, too you?"

Yes, Chanel said, feeling guilty. "Then I think it was that night that I went over to his house, and he ate me out some more. And…"

"And what?"

"I let him perform anal sex on me."

"Chanel!"

"Okay, that's enough!" Bebe said with a stern voice. "Chanel, are you having sex with him?"

"No, that's one thing I won't let him do?"

"Okay, well that's good. Well, you need to cut it off! Chanel, that man is too old for you! Plus, he is taking advantage of you because you are so young. Not to mention, he sounds a bit manipulative. Chanel, you gotta get yourself out of that."

"I don't know-how. I feel bad because my aunt told me a while ago not to get involved with him. As you can see, I didn't listen to her, and now I'm here."

"What did your aunt say?"

"She basically said somethings off about him. I didn't understand why she would say that. He seemed like a nice guy at that time. Now I see what she means."

"Yea, your aunt was right. He's manipulative. He's a stalker. And he is taking advantage of you. It's easy for older men to take advantage of a younger girl. A lot of people think the young lady is at fault. But, he knew what he wanted to do the whole time. You just didn't know."

"I guess you're right. I just feel bad. Whenever I'm over there, I feel bad. In the beginning, it would feel so good, then he starts doing all that stuff."

"What stuff?"

"Like vibrators, dildos, butt plugs."

"Has he used any of these things on you?"

"Yes."

"You didn't think it was weird that a man his age has all those things in his house. Vibrators, butt plugs, dildos?"

"I did. I did. He said he still owned them from a previous relationship."

"And you believed him?"

"I mean, yes. I didn't have no other choice. What am I supposed to believe?"

"Idk girl. Everything about him is sending off red flags! That man is no good for you!"

"I know! You're the first person I told. I haven't even told my best friend. I'm afraid she will judge me. I've been avoiding my aunt. I was supposed to go to church with her and have Sunday dinner, and I'm scared. I'm scared she will know."

"Well, Chanel, even if your aunt does know, so what. She's not going to you. Your aunt loves you. That's why she warned you about him. She knew what he was about. Girl, call your auntie and go to church."

Okay, Chanel said with a blank expression. She felt really bad about her decisions. She felt dirty.

'What's wrong?" Bebe asked.

"It's just that I feel guilty about what I did. I don't like that I'm in this situation."

'Well, we all make mistakes, Chanel Don't feel bad. Don't beat up on yourself. Okay"

"Okay" Chanel said as she turned back to her computer desk. Chanel tried her best to focus on her work. Bebe, who sits next to Chanel, saw how down she was. She got up and rubbed Chanel's back and Chanel smiled. *Today's work day is going to be slower than normal.* The two worked in silence for several hours. Bebe, who stood up to stretch her legs said, "So how is your weave selling business going?"

"I haven't been up with it."

"Really?"

"Yes, really. I'm usually a beast when it comes to selling weave. But I've been distant."

"Mhm. Well, maybe you should get back into it." Bebe encouraged. Chanel knew what Bebe was doing. She was trying to cheer her up and get her back to the old Chanel. The business savvy Chanel. It would take a miracle to get her back there. Chanel looked down at her phone, and it read 10:45. Time seemed to be moving pretty decent. While holding her phone, she thought of her aunt. *Let me give her a call.* Chanel stood up and walked into the bathroom. She pulled her cell phone out and called her aunt.

Ring…ring…ring…

Hello, her aunt answered the phone.

"Hey, auntie," Chanel said.

"Hey baby, how are you! Long time no talk. How is everything?"

"Everything is going good." Chanel lied. She was ashamed to tell her aunt the truth.

"How have things been for you?"

"Well, things have been pretty good. Just getting out in my yard. Nothing fancy."

"Oh, I can imagine your yard work. You've always been pretty thorough."

"Yes, ma'am, you know it." Chanel missed hearing her aunt's voice. She felt a sense of peace come over her.

"Is the offer for the Sunday dinner still on the table?"

"Of course, baby! Why would I take that away?"

"Awesome!"

"Are you still coming to church with me?"

"Sure," she said. Chanel was afraid of going to church. She felt like she didn't belong. She felt that if she walked into the door that everyone would all her business.

"Will you be spending the night? Oh, we can watch movies, eat popcorn, playing board games, just like old-time?" her aunt squealed over the phone. Chanel thought about it. Oh, how she missed her old bed, the smell of her aunt's house, just being in her presence. She would love to be over there and away from Trey. However, Chanel couldn't bring herself to say yes.

"That sounds fun auntie. I work a double today, and I got a few plans tonight after work."

"Oh," her aunt replied through the phone. Chanel felt the somberness in her aunt's voice. Quickly thinking on her toes.

"I'll be at church bright and early, auntie. I'll be you there," Chanel said, trying to cheer her up.

"Yea."

"Well, auntie, I will talk to you later," Chanel replied. She felt the hurt over the phone.

"Okay, babe" see you tomorrow at church.

"See you tomorrow," Chanel hung up the phone and exhaled. She put her head against the wall. She felt terrible. She wanted to with her aunt and play board games like old times, but her spirit wouldn't let her. Shedding a tear. She looked herself in the mirror and tried to find the old Chanel. *Will the real Chanel stand up?* She hung her head low and grabbed a piece of tissue, and wiped away her tears. The objective was to wipe away any evidence that she had been crying, hurt, confused, scared, or unsure. *Hold your head up.* Chanel didn't want anyone knowing that she was hurting on the inside. Masking her pain was an art she learned in her childhood.

She stepped out of the restroom and walked back to her desk.

"Are you okay?" Bebe asked. "You've been gone for a minute?"

"Yes, I'm okay. Everything is fine." Chanel said without even thinking.

"Okay, well, I'm about to go to lunch. Do you wanna come?"

"Yea, that sounds good. I could go for a burger." Both ladies got up and walked to the cafeteria. Chanel relatively quiet. Bebe, noticed a change in Chanel's demeanor.

"Are you sure that everything is okay?"

"Yes, everything is going great. No complaints."

"Okay," Bebe responded. She didn't want to press anymore. The ladies got on the elevator and went to the cafeteria ground floor. The ladies walked around the corridor and entered the cafeteria. Chanel saw a guy that she thought was cute. He worked in a different department than her. He always dressed nice, very polite, and a very infectious smile.

"I think he is so cute, Chanel said to Bebe.

"Who?" Bebe asked. Chanel motioned her head in his direction.

"Don't look, lol. Don't want him to see us looking at him." Bebe looked in the direction Chanel motioned in and saw a nice-looking young man.

"He's cute, Chanel. You should go talk to him."

"Nah, I'm okay."

"Why not?" Bebe asked?

"I just don't think he would like someone like me?"

"What you mean someone like you? What's wrong with you?"

"Nothing, I just don't think that he would like someone like me, that's all. He looks like he has a type."

"You got all that from looking at him?" Bebe asked. Chanel looked at Bebe; then she looked away.

"Don't worry about it."

"I'm not worried. Just concerned. What makes you think that you are unlikeable, unlovable, un-anything?"

"What you mean?"

"I mean, you just basically put yourself down. You don't think he would like a girl like you. I'm trying to understand;

what's a girl like you?" Chanel didn't answer. She didn't know-how. She had a firm belief that guys like him liked certain types of women, and she didn't measure herself up to be that type of woman. So Chanel, unknowingly, gave off mean, b***** vibes and looked closed to other men. She did this as a way to protect herself. However, what she failed to realize was that this behavior is what scares good guys away- Leaving the door open for the mean, manipulative, abusive, and narcissistic types. So when Chanel walked past the guy, she didn't even look in his direction. She just kept walking up to the line to order her food. Bebe, who moved off to the side and was having a conversation with another employee, watch as Chanel avoided looking at the guy. She also noticed the guy's reaction as Chanel walked by. He was indeed reading her. He noticed her, just like she noticed him. Bebe cut her conversation a little short so that she could go stand next to Chanel.

"Hey Chanel girl" Bebe said. "You see anything good on the menu?"

"Uhm, no. I think I'll just stick with my normal."

"Aw okay," Bebe started, "Uhm, you you know that guy was staring at you?"

"What guy?"

"The one you was telling me about. He was staring at you, for a brief moment."

"Oh really?" Chanel said with excitement.

"Yes, but when you walked by him, you looked mean."

"Uh?"

"Yes, you looked mean. You looked closed. You should look more approachable."

"Uh, I hate when people tell that to me. They always tell me that I look unapproachable and that I scare people away, and that I have a resting b**** face, and all this other crap. I don't understand why I *always* have to change my face to appease to other people. What if I'm not in the mood. What if I'm just deeply in my thoughts." She moaned. Bebe, smiled and said, I understand that. I use to do that too at your age. However, I realized that I needed to change. I needed to change my behavior if I wanted to see a change in my circumstances. If you want to attract a quality man Chanel, you have to put off quality energy. Men are good energy readers. They can tell the type of woman they are dealing with. By the way, she walks, carries herself, how she acts, etc."

And, it's okay if you're not interested. You don't have to be interested. You do, need to be ready at all times, though. You never know who you will meet. You never know the type of impression you can leave on somebody. That old saying goes, *"never judge a book by its cover"*, however, we know that ain't true. We are always judging people based on what we see on the outside and not the inside. You've probably walked by some great quality men, and you probably scared them off with your demeanor." Chanel didn't like what Bebe said. It was hard for her to grasp the message. Rightfully so, Chanel was tired of always having to *"change something"* about herself. She felt that people were shallow and entitled. She also believed a lot of what social media said about black girls existing. That black girls can't exist without smiling. That black girls can't exist without being friendly. That black girls can't exist without being approachable. Those black girls can't live without always changing something about themselves. She was tired of this narrative. Tired! Tired! Tired! So Chanel decided to not listen to the advice of Bebe and kept going. She told herself that it didn't matter if she smiled, look friendly, or open because she believed that they would not find her attractive anyway. This was the lie that she told herself every time to excuse her behavior. A lie rooted in low self-esteem, low self-worth, low self-value. Chanel ordered her food and waited off to the side. She wanted to avoid Bebe because the words that Bebe spoke were right. She just wasn't ready to accept it yet. So after her food was ready, Chanel walked to the cashier, paid for her items with some cash because she left her work badge at home, and left Bebe in the cafeteria.

Back upstairs, Chanel was eating at her desk. Bebe appeared from the elevators.

"I was wondering where you disappeared too," Bebe said. Chanel is looking down at her food, avoiding eye contact with Bebe.

"Yes, I was starving. My bad," she lied. But Bebe knew. She knew that Chanel was ruminating over their conversation. So, she let Chanel have her space. Chanel continued to eat her food with her brow furrowed.

The hours past and Chanel did not talk to Bebe. Chanel just occupied herself with her work. When it was time for Bebe to clock out Chanel didn't budge to tell her bye.

"Are you working a double?" Bebe asked.

"Mhm," Chanel answered without evening acknowledging her. Bebe clocked out and came and hugged Chanel. Chanel was so tense. She didn't realize how angry she was. Her face was tight, and her jawline was clinched. Bebe whispered in Chanel's ear,

"I know you're mad at me. Don't think about it. I love you, girl."

"Love you too Bebe," Chanel managed to say. When Bebe left, the weight of Bebe's words weighed on Chanel, and she cried at her desk.

Time had passed quickly after that. Before you knew it, it was time for Chanel to clock out. The time read 10:30 pm. Chanel got up, started breaking down her stuff. She walked to the time clock, ready to clock out, and then she remembered she let her badge at home. *Silly me!* So she just walked on out of the building. She chirped the lock and got into her car.

On her way home, she listened to Jill Scott- The Way. *"Is it the way, you love, me baby"* That is her favorite song by her. It always took her mind off things. Chanel tried to keep herself in a good mood, but she was still pretty bummed. The sourness of all the mistakes she made started to set in. The rape, her suicide attempt, her failed communication with her mother, her weird relationship with her father before he died, her failed relationships, this charade with her neighbor, it all started to boil down on her. Her car ride turned into a nightmare. The tension in her neck rose to her forehead. She tried to take her mind off the pain. But no matter how hard she tried, she couldn't shake it. It plagued her, it annoyed her, it choked her, the pain and anger encapsulated her. She drove that lonely highway with a broken, bleeding heart.

The Favor

"Why me, God?" she yelled at her steering wheel. Her anger surged! *Is this what rock bottom feels like?* Chanel directed her anger towards God!

"It's all your fault," she screamed. *"Why did you let all of this happen to me?"* She felt defeated. She blamed *"Why didn't you protect me?"* she asked through her tears. Chanel pulled into her parking spot outside her condo. She turned the key in the ignition and sat there for what seems like an eternity. She let her seat down and laid back. *I just need to clear my mind.* Then she thought about church. *Ugh, I have to go to this place tomorrow.* Chanel didn't want to. *Why?* Still pissed off, she jerked herself out of the driver seat. She grabbed her things wildly and walked towards the condo building. Not paying attention to her surroundings, Chanel didn't see her younger neighbor walking towards her.

"Hey," he called out to her.

"Hey," Chanel said with an attitude. She didn't see who she was talking to. She didn't stop to look. She just kept walking.

"Is everything okay?" he asked. This pissed Chanel off more. *Ugh, why can't men see that I don't feel like being bothered?.*

"Yes, everything is fine," she started as she turned around. She then realized who she was talking to. She quickly changed her tone.

"I just had a bad day at work." hoping that her attitude didn't scare him off.

"'Aw, okay," he said, as he eyed her. Trying her best to change the subject, "where are you off to?"

"I was going to the building next to yours."

"Aw okay. Going to kick it with one of the other neighbors?"

"Yea, something like that," he answered. "I wanted to apologize about what happened the last time we were out here. I didn't realize you and the ole dude was a couple. I didn't intend to butt in or be disrespectful."

"Oh, you weren't disrespectful at all. We're not a couple."

"You sure?"

"Yea, I'm positive."

"Oh, well, ole dude been telling everybody you're his chick."

"What?" Chanel said in shock. "You can't be serious."

"I'm very serious. He's told everyone here that you all a couple." Chanel felt sick to her stomach. She couldn't believe what she was hearing. *This man is telling everyone that they are a couple.*

"Well, you can go tell everyone that we are not. I promise."

"Lol, okay, he started, "well, you want to get that in check and make sure he knows that."

"I will. Thanks for telling me."

"No problem. What's your name if you don't mind me asking?" "It's Chanel."

"Yours?" "Antoine."

"Nice talking with you, Antoine."

"Nice talking to you too, Chanel. See you around." He said as he walked away. Chanel walked into the building and headed for her door. Before she could make it up the steps, Trey was standing there.

"Hey," she said nervously.

"What's ups?" he asked.

"I'm good. Are you on your way out?"

"Yes, I was. I saw you talking to ole dude," he said sarcastically.

"Yea, we had a fascinating conversation." She said.

"What you all talk about? Me?" he said jokingly.

"Actually, yes, we did talk about you?" she responded.

"Oh?"

"Yea, he told me that you've been going around telling people that were a couple."

"He told you that. I was just joking."

"Really. He seemed convinced that we were a couple."

"Now Chanel, you know I wouldn't do something like that. You can trust me." Trey said. Chanel wasn't buying it.

"Well, I don't want to hold you up," Chanel said as she moved to the side to let him down the steps.

"Aww, it's no big deal. Don't worry about it. I'm just stepping out to my car to grab something."

"Oh, I thought you said you were heading out."

"Yes, but it's kind of late. Plus, you're here. I figured we could keep each other some company."

"Oh, no. I have a church in the morning. I can't be messing around with you tonight?"

"Oh, the church. That's new. Since when you start going back to church?"

"Well, my aunt invited me, and I didn't want to disappoint her."

"I understand and respect that."

"Yea, I need to eat, shower, and get ready for bed."

"Alright. I suppose. I little sad that I can't spend time with you this evening." Chanel rolled her eyes.

"I bet," she responded as she made her way to her door.

"Why you roll your eyes? What I can't want to spend time with you?"

"I didn't say that."

"I know I'm asking."

"I think you're thinking too hard." Chanel turned the key in her lock and opened her door. She turned back to see him eyeing her. "Goodnight, Trey" she said as she closed her door. She made sure that she locked the door behind her. She walked into her bedroom and sat her purse down on her bed. Then afterward, she walked into her kitchen. She reheated leftovers from the other day. She waited in front of the microwave as her food heated up. Like a kid in the candy store, she was excited to eat those shrimp tacos. She took her plate out of the microwave and sat on her bed. She ate her shrimp tacos in one big gulp. *Dang, I was hungry.* She thought to herself. Those shrimp tacos couldn't stand a chance. She threw the plate away and got ready for her shower. She grabbed an oversized shirt and walked into her bathroom. I turned the shower water on full blast and stepped in. The hot water felt like heaven against her skin. She thought about the car ride home. She wasn't okay. She was still hurting. Her heart was still bleeding. She didn't know what to do with this broken heart of hers. She was too tired to do anything about it. She was too tired to talk to God about it. She was tired, overwhelmed, and ready to throw in the towel. *What's the point?.* There were so much anger and pain in her heart. She shuffled out of the shower and turned the water off. She didn't even bother to dry. She just put the t-shirt on. The cold air wrapped around her small frame like a blanket. Chanel looked at herself in the mirror. She looked tired. The once gleaming brown skin girl, looked like she's been through it. *How did I get here?* Then her thoughts shifted to Trey. She felt herself become moist thinking about him. *No! I can not be fooling around with that man! I have a church in the morning.* She walked into her bedroom and plugged her phone in. She looked down at the time. It read 11:45. She knew she needed a night's good rest for a church in the morning. She closed her eyes and eventually fell asleep.

Around 1 am, Chanel was awakened by loud banging on her door. She stumbled out of her bed and was confused. She looked out of the peephole and saw a drunk Trey standing in front of her door. Chanel rolled her eyes and shook her head. *No. I'm not falling for it. I bleed the blood of the Jesus of this mess.* So Chanel walked herself back into her room and laid down in her bed. Another 10 minutes go by, and it's more loud banging. Chanel, feeling annoyed, got up again and saw that it was still Trey beating on her door. As Chanel turned to go back to her bed, Trey called out.

"CHANEL," he shouted. Chanel was pissed. This man picked the perfect time to knock on her door with his drunkenness and harass her before church. Feeling defeated, Chanel decided to open the door. She knew he would not leave her alone. She didn't. She opened the door to see Trey walking back into his apartment. *Shoot!*

"Yes," she answered in a stern voice.

"Did I do something to you?" he asked.

"No, I don't know what you're even talking about?" she said back.

"I'm talking about earlier today. You seemed bothered by me."

"You mean when I came home?"

"Yes."

"No, I'm not upset."

"You sure?" he asked.

"Yes, I'm fine. I think you should get some sleep."

"What if I don't want to go to sleep. What if I want to hold you in my arms?"

"Sorry, that's not an option."

"How come it ain't?"

"Because I said so." Chanel replied. Trey looked her in her eyes as he approached her. Chanel stiffened. Trey got directly in her face.

"Chanel," he said in a deep tone, "I miss you". Chanel instantly became moist. "I'm sorry about the whole thing of me telling people you're my woman. I just like you a lot. I didn't know people were going to take me seriously. Promise! It wasn't intentional."

"Well, idk if I like that, Trey. That's not cool."

"Chanel, you know I like you. You know I will never deliberately try to hurt you". Chanel looked Trey over. He was drunk out of his mind.

"Trey, think you should go back to bed. It's late."

"Okay, I will. Under one condition."

"What's that?"

"Can I have one hug?"

"No."

"Why not?"

"Because you know you go overboard."

"Chanel, it's just one hug. I promise I won't do that extra stuff." Chanel didn't want to hug him. But she knew, if she didn't, he would not leave her alone.

"Can I have a hug? Please!" he asked. Chanel huffed.

"I promise," he said as he walked closer towards her.

"Okay, one hug," Chanel said as she opened her arms. Trey, immediately embraced her. Chanel forgot how good Trey felt. His warmth. His build, His firmness. Chanel found herself at peace. It wasn't long before Trey started caressing Chanel. He began in her upper back as he worked his way down to her lower back, then to her butt. As he rubbed her, he began to plant light kisses along her neck. Chanel couldn't resist. He felt so good. She thought herself tingle in between her legs. She wanted to feel his tongue. Trey sat down on the steps.

"Come here," he motioned to Chanel. She followed his command. He instructed her to place her leg on the step above his head. She listened. He positioned himself under her shirt, and his tongue met her wetness. Chanel moaned in delight. She craved his tongue. He felt so good. She leaned her head back, closed her eyes, and enjoyed the oral sex. Trey cupped her butt and brought her closer to him. He thrust his tongue into her vaginal opening. Chanel spread her legs wider so that he fit his massive tongue inside her. Trey stopped and came from underneath Chanel's shirt.

'Want me to continue?" he asked. Chanel looked down at him also. And his eyes did that weird thing again; they flickered like a flame.

"Uhm, Nah, I'll just go in," she said.

"Why?"

"well, I have a church in the morning."

"Oh, church," he said in a mocking tone.

"Yea, church," she responded. "Is there a problem with that?"

"Nah. It ain't."

"No offense with you, but I don't believe in the white man Jesus". Trey spat. Chanel looked back, stunned.

"Wait, where did that come from. I thought you believed in God?"

"I mean, yea, I use to. But lately, I've been doing a lot of thinking about God, religion, and all of it in it's entirety. I don't believe in God anymore." Chanel couldn't believe what she was hearing. My aunt was right, something is off about him.

"Oh well, I do," Chanel said as she moved her leg down. She became uncomfortable. Trey noticed the shift in her behavior.

"Well, I didn't mean it like that," he said with less emotion in his voice. But still, Chanel wasn't convinced. She knew he was no good. But yet even she entertained his foolishness.

"Okay, well, I have to go now," Chanel replied as she walked back to her condo door. Trey grabbed her by the hand.

"Wait, I'm sorry. I didn't mean to offend you," as he drew her in. He pulled her close to his body and held her. Chanel huffed. She didn't want this. She didn't want him. She didn't want any of this. She wished she never met him.

"C'mon Chanel, don't be like that," he said softly in her ear. He began to slow dance with her in the hallway.

He caressed her body as he planted soft kisses on her neck. Her knees began to buckle. He slowly moved his fingers to the front and started rubbing on her sweet spot in between thighs. Chanel felt herself sinking deeper into this never-ending hole of pleasure. He continued to rub her through her shirt. His light kisses turned into slow licks and, tongue kisses on her neck. He was irresistible. As he massaged her through her shirt, he began to finger her through her through her shirt. The fabric entering her acted as a barrier and provided a new sensation. She liked it. He pushed her against the door. With his other hand he slid his hand down underneath her panties and started rubbing her clit. Chanel gasped. He kneeled down and began to kiss her nipples through her shirt. Biting, licking, teasing, sucking. He brought one finger up and stuck it in her mouth. Chanel has never tasted her own juices. This was all a new feeling to her. He then kneeled down and moved and once again positioned himself under her shirt for a second time and made love to her sweet spot with his tongue until she climaxed over, over, and over again.

The next day at church, Chanel felt dirty. It was hard for her to keep her focus on what the preacher was saying. All she could think about was last night with Trey. How she once again fell for his trap and how good his tongue felt. She was embarrassed. She knew dang well, that man was no good for her, and knew she needed to end it. But I didn't know-how. Chanel stared off in space. She was searching her thoughts for a solution to her problem. *Okay, I need to focus.* She urged herself to pay attention in church.

"See, Eve allowed the serpent to change her perception about the apple in the garden," the pastor started.

"Eve knew that the apple was bad. For God had given the command to not eat from the tree of knowledge of good and evil. Because if they eat its fruit, you are sure to die. See, the problem with Eve was, what did God say? Often, the enemy will trick us because we listen to what God said. We have our interpretation of what God said. The enemy heard the command of God. He heard exactly what God told Adam about eating from the tree of knowledge of good and evil. When the serpent tested Eve's knowledge of what God said, she gave her spin of it. Proving she didn't hear it. God said, don't eat from the tree of knowledge of good and evil. If you eat its fruit, you are sure to die. See, the enemy asked if God "really" say you must not eat the fruit from any of these trees in the garden? Notice, God never said that. He gave one specific command. He rephrased God's command so that she didn't detect the trap he was setting up for her. Eve answers confidently, saying "Of course we may eat fruit from the trees in the garden. It's only the fruit from the tree in the middle of the garden that we cannot eat. She further says that God told them not to touch it or eat it because they will die. How often we experience this in life? How many times has God-given us specific commands about a person, places, and things only for us to disobey him because of our lust? Eve lusted the apple, it was made to seem good in her site. But when she and her mate took a bite of the apple, they realized the terrible mistake they made. Their eyes were indeed open. And they covered themselves in shame. There is someone in this room right now in the battle of their life because they struggle between what God said and forbidden fruit, being made to look good in their site. IF only they would open their mouth and ask for help. For God said he would fight your battles for you!"

Chanel froze in her pew. *Oh my, he's talking to me. He's talking about me.* Chanel begun to feel guilty in the church. She knew the preacher was speaking about her situation with her neighbor. She knew he was no good for her. She knew he was manipulative, he was charming, and he was seductive. The way he would caress her body. The way he kissed her neck. The way his tongue felt between her thighs made her knees instantly buckle. Chanel knew she needed to be delivered from his grasp. But she was afraid to ask. How can she ask for help? Especially after she lied to her aunt. She wanted help badly, but somebody shamed her.

The preacher began the prayer call. "I'm calling all of the deacons and pastors to form a line so that individuals may come down and receive prayer. As they line up, give each of them a tube a holy oil." Chanel felt a cold shiver go down her spine. *Oh no, not a deliverance call.* Chanel was mortified by deliverance calls. She's always seen them on tv or when visiting someone else church. People will get hands laid on them and fall out. Chanel felt nervous about doing that type of worship. That wasn't her style. She was more of a quiet worshipper very private moment between her and God.

"If that sermon is about you, please come down to the alter so that we may pray for you. Please do not feel discouraged. Do not feel ashamed. Do not feel embarrassed. There is no condemnation in the Lord," the pastor started. Chanel looked around the church, checking to see if anyone else felt his message in the spirit. No one else seemed to be budging. Chanel slightly sunk in her seat. She felt a small tap on her shoulder. She turned to see her aunt looking at her.

"Yes, auntie," she replied

"Are you alright, dear?" her aunt asked.

"Yes, ma'am," she started.

"Are you sure?" as she studied Chanel's face. Chanel nodded her head, yes. And turned her gaze back towards the front. The music blared in the church as the deacons and pastors waited for someone to come and get deliverance. Chanel sat in her seat quietly. She was fighting the urge to go up there. She wanted healing. But she didn't want to feel exposed in front of all these people. She didn't want everyone to know what she's been doing with her neighbor at different times of the day. She felt another tug on her clothing. She looked over, and her grandmother replied

"Chanel, if you need someone to go up there with you, I can?"

"Huh?" Chanel responded

"If you need someone to walk up to the altar with you, I can," she repeated.

'What makes you think I should walk up to the altar?"

"Chanel, you don't think I know that you are still in communication with your neighbor? I mean, you came to church late this morning. And you just really haven't been yourself. You've been lying to me about him. I was young once. I understand. But, I know that man is no good for you. And when the pastor was preaching about Eve in the garden, I couldn't help but think that he was talking about you. You are eve in this current situation, and your neighbor is the forbidden fruit. Don't be afraid, Chanel; God loves you. And yes, our human nature will make him upset with us. But know he is here waiting for you to come clean and to help you." Chanel froze and became teary-eyed at her aunt's words. *How in the world did she know she was lying about her neighbor? Was it that obvious?* Chanel squeezed her aunt hand and stood up. Her aunt stood up with her. And she walked down the aisle.

"Thank you, God. For this brave soul as they make their way to the altar" Chanel tried lowering her head in shame.

"please feel the shameful, child. God is not angry with you. He is correcting you. He is setting you free from the bondage. He is healing you. He is delivering you." As Chanel made her way to the altar to receive deliverance on her current situation, she saw that others too finally got out of their seats to receive prayer. Chanel walked up to a woman pastor with short gray hair cut into a bob. She smiled at Chanel and hugged her. She rubbed holy oil on Chanel's hand and stood in agreement. As the older woman began praying, Chanel felt a powerful force that made her legs give out...

Chanel helped out in her aunt's kitchen cooking yams, greens, cornbread, and fried chicken for Sunday dinner.

"It should' smell good in here!" Chanel joked. Her aunt bumped hips with her and said,

"It still does doesn't it" in her Mississippi accent. Both of the women laughed and giggled as their humor and light spirit filled the air. Chanel started stirring the green pot making sure they don't burn at the bottom. She caught her aunt looking at her through her peripheral vision.

"Yes, auntie," Chanel started as she turned to face her. Her aunt smiled and said,. "You know, I know you've had a very rough life. And everything that you've been through with your mom, your dad, and you come to live here. Life was not fair to you. Yet, Chanel, here you are, making progress through everything. And I couldn't be prouder of you". Her aunt looked. Chanel became teary-eyed at her aunt's speech. "Chanel, I don't want anything bad to happen to you. I pray to God every single day on your behalf. Chanel, girl, I love you so much. And I know my daughter was not the best mother to you. And I feel guilty every day I think about the day you had to move here with me. Baby, if I could take it back, I would! If I could try to trade places with you, I would! Chanel, you are my heart! I love you to infinity and back." She embraced Chanel tightly in the kitchen. Both women sobbed uncontrollably on each-others arms."

"I love you auntie," Chanel managed in-between her sobs.

"I love you too, baby, I love you too". Suddenly the smoke detector went off!

"The chicken, it's burning, Chanel yelled. Chanel's aunt quickly turned the stove off as Chanel grabbed a towel and fanned the smoke alarm.

"Looks like we won't be having fried chicken," her aunt said. Both women laughed. "Let's eat."

Chanel made it home about 9:30 that night from her aunt's house. It felt perfect to spend time with her. She adored her aunt, and she loved her so much. Chanel knew her aunt cared deeply for her and wanted nothing but the best for her. She was grateful to have such a woman like her in her life. Chanel parked her car and observed her condo. It was peaceful. She was happy to have a place of her own finally, but she knew her neighbor would not let up. Chanel's body felt weak when he was around. She craved his touch. He felt so good. She knew she had to put a stop to this. So Chanel came up with her way to free herself. Hopefully, he would understand. She exited her car, locked the door behind her, and entered the building. Chanel quietly approached her neighbor's door and knocked.

"Who is it" he called out.

"it's me, Chanel". Trey opened the door with the biggest grin on his face. "Well, hello beautiful, you look very nice today" as he looked Chanel up and down, licking his lips.

Hey Trey, I need to talk to you about something.

"Okay"

'Well, I think it's time we stop these favors. It's just that It's not right in the eyes of God and I don't want to jeopardize my relationship with him in any way". Chanel finished her comment and waited for him to reply. He was neutral, and it was hard to read. They stood in silence for several minutes before he finally answered.

"Okay, I understand," he said.

"Really?"

"Yes, I remember yesterday that you said you were going to church. And I noticed your reaction to me saying

I don't believe in God anymore. I didn't mean to offend you, and I respect your wishes."

"Wow, okay," Chanel was shocked. She didn't know it was going to be that easy. "Okay, that's all I wanted; I didn't want to take up too much of your time."

"Okay, thank you for being honest with me; I appreciate that."

"No problem."

"One more thing, before you go."

"What's that?"

"Can I have one last hug? I promise I won't do anything extra."

"Uhm, no, I don't think that's appropriate," Chanel responded. Trey's face turned into a frown. He became furious at her. He lowered his head and demanded in an angry voice.

"Why not?"

"Because I said so, Chanel responded. She is becoming tired of him continually questioning her as to why she said no.

"You act like don't trust me or something. Remember, all I want is for you to be comfortable."

You always say you want to make me comfortable. But when I tell you, no, you still proceed to do what you want. That's not fair to me."

"Chanel, I wouldn't do anything to hurt you" Trey pleaded.

"Trey, can you stop making this about you. This is what I want, and this is what I'm comfortable with."

"Alright," Trey threw his hands up in a defensive motion.

"Look, Trey, I'm sorry. But this is what makes me comfortable not hugging you. You tend to always take advantage of me." Chanel had it. "I'm sorry, but we can't hug, touch, or kiss. Hopefully, you can understand that." Chanel backed away slowly and turned away to go to her condo. When she looked over her shoulder, Trey still stood in the doorway with an unreadable expression. She walked into her condo and closed the door shut.

The Blame Game

Flashes back

"Welcome Chanel, how are things going for you?"

"Things are going good. However, I keep having these moments where my past comes back into my mind."

"How so?" "Well, I see and hear the things people say to me. I see how that hinders me today." "Can you be more specific?"

"Okay, I hear my mother saying these horrible things to me. Like for example, I wanted to go to school for writing. I loved writing. It was my passion. I wanted to explore that side of me deeper. Well, when I went and told her what it was that I wanted, she told me "No!" She continued to say that, "people don't get good jobs in writing. You have to go to school for something in the science department. You have to go to school in a career where you can support yourself. Being a scientist is a better choice. I pleaded with her and said, that's not what I want to do; I want to go to school for writing. She told me no! That I cannot go to school for writing; it was forbidden. I will only go to school for a career in science.

"How did that make you feel?' "I was upset. I was so upset with her. I couldn't believe that she shot down my dream in science. This is what I wanted so bad. I was crushed." "How is this affecting you now?"

Because, I'm unhappy with a lot of my choice. I feel like I'm constantly looking for my mother's approval for everything. I feel stuck. And I also feel like that's the reason why I majored in science major because of what my mother wanted." "How old are you, Chanel?" "I'm 18 going on 19.""How old were you when this happened?" "I was 12 or 13 years old." "I see, so about 5-6 years ago." "Yes."

"Okay, Chanel, you can do anything you want now. You are in control of yourself. You are in control of your life. Only you from this point one can say what stays and what goes." "Huh?"

"I'm saying that it's unfortunate that your mother made you feel that way, and you all didn't see eye on a particular situation. However, Chanel, you are in control now. Suppose you want to pursue a career in writing. Do it." Chanel felt her face getting tight. She was pissed. She felt that the therapist didn't understand that her mother was controlling. That if she didn't follow her mother's wishes, that she will be disappointing her.

"You don't understand."

"Understand what?" "Understand that I can't just go to school for writing. That I have to stay with this stupid science stuff." "That's what I'm saying, Chanel. You are in control. If you don't want to do science, just don't do science. What does it matter what your mother says?"

"Because she will be pissed off at me if I did something different."

"Okay. So you are afraid of what your mother says? You are afraid of her being upset that you choose something for you?"

"No, I'm not afraid of what my mother says. I want to honor what she says?"

"In honoring what she says, Chanel, you are going against what you want? Why do you seek approval from your mother?" "What?' "Why do you do seek approval from your mother?"

"I'm not seeking approval."

"Yes, you are. You are seeking her to validate you. To validate your dreams. To validate your life. To validate your existence. Don't you see that your mother will not support you in this way? She has already made her mind up because of her fears. However, Chanel you have the power to change the trajectory of your life. Suppose you would just take control of what of it. You don't have to follow through with a science degree if you don't want to. You choose."

"But I am choosing."

"I'm choosing to follow her directions. I'm just saying, her directions what is causing my life to be miserable now." "No, Chanel, she's not making your life miserable. You are making your life miserable. Because you choose too."

"No, no, no, it's all here. Like for example. I said I wanted to go to school to become a doctor. My grandmother told me that was dumb. She said that I was stupid for even considering it. That I was selfish to think of it. She told me to think of all the debt that I would be putting my mother through if I did something like that."

"Okay, how old were you when she said this?" "Around the same age. I did this career test thing at school. You know where they figure out what are your strongest suits. Or what career would you likely go into? I did well in both science and communication. I choose communication. My family choose science. So I did science because that's what they wanted me to do." "That was then Chanel. You were a kid. I'm sorry for what happened to you. However, you have the power now to decide for you. So go and pick the career you want.""It's not that easy. I don't want to disappoint them.""Right, you want them to validate you. At the same time, you pursue a degree in an area that you don't love. Then you get to blame them for it.""I'm not blaming them. They are the reason that I am here.""No, Chanel you are the reason you are here. You don't have to go through with science if you don't want too. Simply choose something different." Chanel huffed. She felt her chest become tight. She felt her jawline tighten. She started to feel hot in her chair. Then she started shaking her looking down. The hot tears rolled down her face. She refused to believe that she was the reason that she was there. No, it was her mother's fault. No, it was her family's fault. They made her do this, and now she's suffering from the pain of this. She wanted freedom. She wanted to do the writing, but she knew that she couldn't do writing because her mother would disapprove of it.

"Chanel, what makes you so afraid to go after your dreams? Are you afraid that your mother will be upset with you? They are your dreams. Not hers. It's your life.

Not hers. Your mother does not have any control over you anymore. Chanel, you are free. Can't you see that? You are keeping yourself in bondage. You have to step outside of the victim mentality. You have to see yourself as the winner you truly are. Chanel, you are stronger than you imagine. You are powerful. However Chanel, you have to see that for yourself. No one else can see it for you. You have to believe that for you. You have to want that for you. If not, you will continue to rely on others to affirm your identity. You are born and designed for a purpose. IF your purpose is writing, go for it. You have the power to make that choice now. You've been waiting for people to show up in your life. You've been waiting for someone or something to come along and affirm your dreams, your goals, your aspirations in life. You have been waiting for approve your life. Chanel, only you can approve your life. Only you can move forward if you want to. Only you can do that. Only It's okay Chanel, if you make your mother upset. And you don't have to change your decisions because she's upset. Yes, you had to respect her wishes then. However, respecting her wishes doesn't mean you don't get to choose what's right for you. Now is the time for you, Chanel to take back control over your life and pick what you feel is appropriate for you. You are the co-creator of your life. You are in charge of what stays and what goes. You have a say. Use your voice and dictate what stays and what goes. You are exactly everything you need. The affirmation that you are seeking can only come from you. Only you!"

Chanel looked down at the floor in irritation. She did not want to accept what the therapist said because all her mind could say was, "It's their fault."

Chanel sat on her bed.

"Today it feels a little crappy." Chanel sat on her bed. She was in a bad mood. She couldn't detect why, but she was. *Something is off.* So she stood up and walked into the bathroom. She looked herself over in the mirror and wondered about Trey. She wanted to escape from her mood today and go over and let him do "it." But she knew she shouldn't because A. he is no good for her, B. It's not right in the eyes of the Lord, C. she needed freedom from this demon. She exhaled and braced herself on the sink. As she closed her eyes and rotated her neck in a circular motion, her phone chimed. Chanel opened her eyes and quickly walked back into her bedroom, and checked her phone. It was Courtney.

"Hey, girl," Chanel texted back.

"Hey, how are you?"

"I'm doing good. Yourself?" "I'm doing okay. I wanted to check on you. I haven't spoken to you in a while, wanted to make sure you were okay."

"Yea, I'm fine." "Are you sure?"

"Yes. I do appreciate you checking on me, though. I was having sort of a tough day."

"Oh really, what's going on?" Courtney asked. Chanel was hesitant. *Should I tell Courtney the truth?"* she wondered.

"How are you and that neighbor of yours?" Courtney asked.

"Interesting, you ask. Things are okay."

"Really now?" "Yea, things are okay." Chanel was afraid of being judged by Courtney. Courtney was her best friend since grade school.

"Wanna come over?"

"Sure. I'm free today."

"Can you come over now?"

"Uhm, yea, I can. Is everything alright?"

"Yes, I will tell you when you get here."

"Okay." Chanel dropped her phone on the bed and laid back against the headboard. She took a deep breath. As she waited for Courtney to come over, she started imaging how she would respond.

"What's your address?"

"1225 Blackjack Lane."

"Okay, I will be there in 15 minutes." Chanel felt herself get a bit anxious. She opened her laptop and logged into her student account. When she saw her grades she was shocked. Her A in chemistry dropped down to a C+, her A in biochemistry dropped to a C-, and her A in microbiology dropped to a D.

"Omg," she shrieked. She couldn't believe that her grades dropped tremendously. She just couldn't believe it. So then she started looking at her scores. Chanel realized that she missed several assignments from each class, and she scored poorly on the latest quizzes. *Following behind Trey and not doing my work, my grades are falling.* She got pissed. It's unlike her to get bad grades in anything. She is a star student. She also found an email from her chemistry teacher.

Good Evening Chanel,

I've noticed that your grade has dropped two letter grades in class. I usually don't reach out to students on their performance. However, yours is quite striking. I've also noticed that your quiz scores have been low, and you've missed several assignments. I am free to talk about what's going on and help you get back on track. I want to see you do well. If you need to reach me, you can text my cell number found in the syllabus or scheduled office hours. I'm worried about you.

Sincerely,
Dr. Pincher

Chanel hung her head low. She felt defeated that her grades had dropped so low and that she was doing poorly in all of her classes. Just as she was about to respond to Dr. Pincher's email, Courtney called. Chanel quickly answered her phone. "Hey, girl." "Hey, I'm pulling into the condo complex. Which is your door?" "I'm door A on the first floor."

"Okay, cool, I'm about to park." Chanel got off her bed and walked to her front door. She opened it and waited for Courtney to come inside. The main door opened, and Courtney walked up the steps and found Chanel standing in the doorway.

"Hey girl," Courtney greeted Chanel.

"Hey girl," Chanel said, trying her best to mask her energy.

"I'm so excited to see your place." "Yea, this is your first time here isn't it."

"Yes. Can I have a tour?" "Of course." Chanel gave Courtney a tour of the condo. Courtney fell absolutely in love with Chanel's condo. It was so cute and befitting for her friend. Chanel, on the other hand, was trying her best to conceal her frustrations. She put on her best fake smile. However, Courtney was a master of reading people's emotions.

"What wrong, hun? You seem off?" Chanel just burst into tears. "Courtney, I've done something terrible."

"What's that?" Courtney said as she consoled her friend. Courtney walked her friend over to the couch, and both ladies sat down. Courtney rubbed Chanel's head.

"Courtney, I've been letting my neighbor do sexual stuff to me." "What kind of sexual stuff?"

"Well, it first started with him comforting me. Then it evolved to him performing oral sex on me. Now, I let him have anal sex with me. And I feel disgusting."

"Oh, Chanel!"

"I know Courtney, I know. I've been letting him do these things to me. I feel horrible. I know it's wrong. But it's like I can't stop myself. Sometimes Courtney, I genuinely don't want to do anything with him. But then he asks me for a hug. This hug is not no ordinary hug. He feels on my body; he kisses my neck, he feels good. I end up falling for his hugs, and that lead to him performing oral sex on me. Then when I do try to fight back about his hugs, he makes me feel guilty and says things like, "I just want you to be comfortable, or you can trust me, or you act like going to hurt you and take advantage of you. Courtney, it's a never-ending cycle. I can't pull myself out of this. Then I feel guilty because sometimes I do crave his tongue. I feel sick. I don't know what to do."

"Chanel, you are innocent. This man is taking advantage of you. He's using his hugs as a way to lure you in. It's like a lion stalking his prey. You are his lunch. It reminds me of that bible scripture says the enemy prowls around like a roaring lion looking for something to devour. When you watch the lion in the wild, who do they go after? The weak, the sick, and the young. He knows you are too young, and he goes after you because you are an easy target. But don't feel guilty for falling into his trap. You didn't know what he had up his sleeve. You just wanted to be nice and wanted a friend."

"Right. I forgot to mention he followed me to school."

"HE WHAT" "He followed me to school. Like literally came to my school and stood in the cafeteria." **"OMG, HE'S A PREDATOR. CHANEL, YOU MUST STOP TALKING TO HIM. IF HE FOLLOWS YOU TO SCHOOL, THERE IS NO TELLING WHAT ELES HE IS CAPABLE OF."**

"Courtney, I don't know what to do. I told him yesterday that I'm over letting him do nasty stuff to me. But today, I woke up wanting it."

"It's a demonic attack, Chanel. The enemy is tempting you to go back. He is trying to prove to God that you are a liar and not to believe your words. It's an attack. You must fight back, Chanel."

"I know, but it's hard because keep remembering all this stuff that happened to me in the past; the rape, my relationship with my parents, everything. I feel like my circumstances are the reason why I am here. I don't feel like I'm in the right frame of mind."

"Chanel, don't talk like that. Just because it happened in your past doesn't mean it has to be your future. Chanel, you can change the trajectory of your life."

"No, I can't. I have too much stuff inside me, like with Andrew. I remembered that I let Andrew rape me because he made me feel guilty. He made me feel that I was doing something wrong if I didn't give him what he wanted. So I let him rape me. And I know I'm letting Trey do the same thing."

"Chanel, you can't keep holding on to the past. First thing, you didn't let Andrew rape you. He raped you and took advantage of you. He disrespected your boundaries and only cared about himself. Andrew lied to you Chanel. It is not your fault what Andrew did. Stop blaming yourself and stand in authority. Tell your past that it no longer has control over you anymore." "Okay, what about my dad?' "What about him?"

"He's also the reason why I'm in this pardictment. He wouldn't take accountability for his actions. I always took for him. What I didn't realize was he was the culprit. He caused hurt and pain to me too. He hurt me too. I also don't hold Andrew responsible. I didn't hold Trey accountable. These men are hurtful, and I take up for them. Don't you see, I'm a wreck! How can you expect me to release my past? All these men are hurting me."

"Chanel, you have to choose your healing. It doesn't come easy. You have to make the mental choice to heal. God gives us deliverance. However, you have to heal and heal by letting it go and moving on. You are keeping yourself in this prison in your mind." Chanel became very upset. The words Courtney spoke reminded her of what the psychologist said many months ago. Chanel did not believe that this healing Courtney told of her responsibility.

"No," Chanel said defensively. "No, I refuse to believe that they don't have to take any accountability for how I turned out. It's their fault. Here you are telling me to let it go. You've never been raped. You didn't have to deal with that pain. You have no clue what you speak of. Courtney, you're supposed to be my friend. You sound just like that psychiatrist. This conversation is over." Chanel said in an angry tone. Courtney just looked at her friend. Her eye was sadden with disbelief. She knew that for Chanel to heal truly from her past, Chanel would have to make the mental decision to want to. This conversation is pointless. Courtney stood and said, "Well, it seems like you made up your mind." Courtney walked to the door looking down at the ground. Chanel felt defeated. She walked behind her friend in a sunken mood. Courtney opened the door and let herself out. "Chanel, I'll be praying for you. I believe, that if you want to heal, you will do what is necessary." Courtney turned and walked out of the building. Chanel stood in the hallway, sad, depressed, angry, mad, and bitter. She couldn't focus. *God, please help me. Please!* She walked back into her condo. Then suddenly, this voice popped into her head and instructed her to reach out to Andrew. *Make him accountable*, the voice demanded. So Chanel went and grabbed her phone and started searching for Andrew's number. It's been a long time since she's talked to him. She saved his number in her phone for all these months because she knew that this would happen one day. She finally found his number protected under his initials, A.M., which stands for Andrew Morrison.

"Andrew," she started the text. She didn't know what to say. Her emotions were all over the place. She focused her thoughts on what to say. How she would say it and how she would respond to his denial.

"Yes," he texted back. "Chanel, is this you?"

"Yes"

"What's up?" "Well, I wanted to talk to you about something." "Okay?"

"Well, it's about what you did to me. I don't know if you know this, but ever since that day you raped me, my life has turned upside down. I've been depressed, suicidal and had to see a counselor because the impact was so great. I've lost my confidence, and it has taken so much to get it back. I'm not functioning the way I use to. Andrew, you hurt me when you took advantage of me that day. You know I didn't want to have sex, and you did it anyway because all you cared about was you. It was never about me. It was all about you. And what bothers me more is to see you live your life as if nothing happened. Here you are in another relationship, graduated college, and living your best life, while I'm still trying to piece together what is left of me. It's not fair, and I just want old Chanel to come back. My life has literally turned upside down. Yes, I have my own hair business, a nice condo, and I'm soon graduating college. But Nah, you are living your life like you didn't rape someone. Like you didn't cause pain to someone. Like you didn't wreck someone's life. I feel like you owe me." Chanel's face was tight. She was mad as hell and waited for him to reply. She hoped that he would take accountability for what he did, and maybe he would have some resolve to himself. But nope, instead, he texted back, "Chanel, I thought we had consensual sex. I'm sorry if my behavior and actions hurt you. That was not my intention. I didn't know that what happened between us bothered you so greatly. Once again, I'm sorry if I hurt you." Chanel was pissed. *How dare he say, "if"*. She had to control her anger any longer.

"You know what, when I texted you, I was expecting you to have some resolve about yourself. But no. Instead, you continue to prove yourself to be the low life piece of s*** I always knew you would end up to be. First of all, there is no if! You did it! Did I not say that I did not want to have sex? Did I not express explicitly that I didn't feel comfortable doing that to you? And most importantly, DIDN'T I EXPRESS I DID NOT WANT TO HAVE SEX WITH YOU? DID I NOT? DID I NOT? DID I NOT? Newsflash Andrew, when a woman says that she does not want to have sex, they mean it. It's not rocket science. You lied to me, you took advantage of me, and you refuse to accept accountability for what you have done. I hope you haven't done this to your new girlfriend. You are sick, and I hope you rot in hell!" Andrew texted back immediately.

"I'm sorry Chanel, that I hurt you. I never meant to. I've learned a lot from this conversation. I would be cliché to ask for forgiveness, but that's the only thing I can do. I wish I can take back the past and erase my wrongs. I'm sorry that you have been carrying this burden. I'm sorry, Chanel, I don't know what else to say." Chanel responded.

"Sorry, ain't good enough". She threw her phone on the other side of the room and screamed to the top of her lungs. She ran chaotically to her bed and flung herself down hard. Hot tears rolled down her face as she lay in a fetal position. She rocked back and forth, back and forth. *God, please help me!* Then she cried herself to sleep.

Fight Back

"Did you know that most Christians don't read their bibles? The devil-like it's when you are a believer. You are only a threat if you read your bible".

Chanel woke up in the middle of the night, entangled by her desires. She wanted Trey. She wanted to feel his tongue in between her thighs. She tried to escape what she was dealing with. She didn't realize that she was using Trey to distract her from the growing problem that was becoming too much to bear. Trey was a sweet escape. He melted her problems away like ice on a flame. But it's met with incredible guilt because she knows she's not supposed to be there, she knows he is toxic to her, she knows that he manipulates her, she knows that he guilts her, she knows, *she knows*. Yet, she can't pull herself out of this trap. She wants too. She's having trouble fighting back. In her mind, fighting back is hard. Fighting back requires work. Fighting back means people will be angry with you. She still remembers all the pain she felt growing up. She still remembers the pain of her mother. She still remembers the rape. She remembers all of the bad things that has happened to her thus far and how each one plays a role in her situation today. In Chanel's mind, she is the victim.

So it caught her totally by surprise when a voice said: "write."

"Huh?' Chanel said out loud. She thought she was crazy. She tried to focus her attention on something else. Again the voice said, *"write!"* Chanel was confused. She didn't understand what was happening to her. She sat up on the side of her bed, still tired. She hung to the side of the bed as she gathered her thoughts. She didn't understand what she needed to write about. But still, the voice insisted that she writes. Chanel didn't want to write. She didn't know why she needed to. She wanted freedom from Trey, deep down, she does, but her body, this thing she cannot control, is pushing her towards him. Chanel searched every avenue in her mind as a possible solution. She didn't know how to give her problems to God. Maybe he won't listen to what I have to say. She wanted to fight this thing on her own; however, it was wearing her out. Puff up with pride, Chanel couldn't bring herself to open her mouth and ask God for help. In her memory, she remembered that many Christians die in their pain because they refuse to ask for help. God did not create you to handle your problems by yourself. It is a "we" factor. She sat silent on the side of her bed. She felt a strong tug on her heart to ask for help .What she considered to be her weakest moment was her strongest.

Dear Lord,

It's me again. I know I've done some questionable things as of recently. I was unaware of how my behavior could lead to something like this. Something that I considered harmless has turned into a total nightmare Lord. Please first and foremost forgive me, Father. Thank you for sending your son Jesus Christ to die on the cross for my sins. You made me clean and whole. You gave me a new life. You gave me hope. I'm forever grateful. Now, Lord, I need your help. I'm in this sticky situation with this man whose manipulative. I got myself into this thing with this man, that I cannot seem to get out of. When I try to turn away, he pulls me back. He makes me feel guilty. I feel powerless. Lord, what is the missing piece to the puzzle? Lord, reveal to me what it is that I'm missing. How can I heal from this situation? In Jesus's name Amen.

Chanel sat on the side of the bed, feeling defeated. Tears rolled down her face. She rocked back and forth, back and forth. Then finally the voice said again,

"Write". She realized it was The Lord talking to her. So Chanel got up and grabbed a piece of paper and a pencil from her bookbag. She sat back down on her bed.

"Okay", she started, "write about what?"

"Your father," the voice said.

"My father?" Chanel answering The Lord back, "write about him, what about him. I barely know him," she scoffed. She became angry. *Why must I write about a man I barely know?* Chanel stared at the paper. Nothing came to her. Nothing. Then she realized, well, maybe I can write about this. So Chanel began writing about her dad. The nothingness that she felt.

"Well, God told me to write about you. But I don't know what. I guess I can write about this, what I'm feeling at this moment, which is nothing. You were never there for me. You left me. You abandoned me. I use to look for you. But you were too busy living your life being a dope boy. I remember a few times I would see you as a kid, with your fancy cars, and you call me to you. You would give me a piece of candy, some money, maybe even some shoes. But I wanted more. I wanted you to love me. I wanted you to ask me about my day. How come you never asked me about my day? How come you never asked me what school was like? How come you never knew that Mommie and me struggled? How come you didn't rescue me? Did I matter to you? Did you care about me? I cared about you! Dad, I loved you, and you treated me like crap. There's more to a child than buying them clothes and shoes. What about emotional bonding. Physical bonding. I don't think I ever hugged you. Do you know what it feels like to me knowing that I never hugged you? It hurts. I'm mad at you. I'm angry at you. Yea, I use to get those stupid letters you sent me. And yes, I didn't respond. You reached out to me because why you feeling guilty? No! You don't get to pick me up when you feel like it. I wish you were never my Dad."

Chanel slammed her pen down and got into the fetal position. She held herself as she cried. She was so angry at her dad for leaving her with that terrible mother of hers. Chanel continued to cry hard tears.

"I HATE THEM! BOTH OF THEM! THEY ARE THE REASON WHY I'M GOING THROUGH THIS. IT'S THEIR FAULT," she screamed at the top of her lungs. Her face became tight; her, jaw clenched, veins popping out of her neck, heavy breathing, her eyes blared. Chanel began to rock back and forth, trying to console herself. Nothing was working. She was so dang on angry. The more she tried to forget, the more she kept remembering the offense. It was like a movie scene. When one location ended, a new one appeared. Then another voice said, *"See how they treated you. You should curse them"*. Chanel heard the voice. And she thought about it for a while. But another voice kept telling her, *"forgive."* She became confused. She didn't know what to do. One voice was telling her to curse her parents while another voice instructed her to forgive her parents. Chanel answered the agent who told her to ignore,

"Why should I forgive them? Look at what they did to me. Did you see how they treated me? And you want me to forgive them?"

Chanel was hot. She didn't understand. So she just laid there in her bed, angry. She stared at the ceiling for what seemed liked ages. Chanel laid in her bed and slowly started to drift off to sleep. As she drifted deeper and deeper into her slumber, the same voice that initially told her to write about her father and forgive him spoke to her again,

"Chanel," the voice said gently.

"Yes," she answered back.

"Forgive," the voice urged her in a gentle yet stern tone. Chanel woke up again. This time she was saddened by the instructions of the agent. She realized it was The Lord

who spoke to her and was upset because she didn't want to forgive her dad. She reached down and picked up her cell phone and dialed her friend Courtney.

Ring ring ring... No answer. So she called again, ring... ring...ring... Still no answer. Chanel just sat there with her emotions torn. She knew she had to forgive her dad because the Lord instructed her to; at the same time, she didn't want to. She wanted him to be responsible. In her mind, she thought forgiving her father means letting him off the hook. In her mind, she thought he needed to be held accountable for the pain and suffering he caused her. In her mind, it was his fault. *I just couldn't bear forgiving him.* Even now, as an adult. Every time she thought about ignoring him, she was reminded of all the pain he caused her.

"I wish I had someone to talk to. Anyone. But whose awake at this hour?" Chanel sat in the middle of her bed, head pressed against her knees. She needed relief. She wanted something to help take her mind off this situation. Then the thought of Trey popped into her head. Without even thinking, Chanel got up and walked to her front door. She walked up the steps and knocked on Trey's door. She waited. No reply. She knocked again. Still no reply. She huffed, *"what am I doing?"* As she made her way across the down the steps, the Lord said,

"You keep going around this same mountain. How can you ask for freedom when you keep coming over here?"

Chanel felt guilty. The Lord was right. She asked for deliverance but yet walked right into the lion's den. Then the story of Eve and the serpent popped into her head. She hurried quickly into her apartment and closed the door.

She didn't want to risk the chance of running into Trey. She locked the door behind her and sat on her bed. With her hands pressed into the mattress, she started rocking back and forth, back and forth. *Why is this so hard?* She said to herself. She threw herself on the bed, and she heard a knock at the door. Chanel sat up. *OMG*. She knew it had to be Trey. She tiptoed quietly to the door and looked through the peephole. It was Trey. He had on a t-shirt and grey pajama bottoms. Chanel eyed him through the peephole. He looked amazing as the light illuminated off him. She instantly felt herself getting wet. Her inner thoughts screamed, **"it's a test. It's a test!"**. Chanel knew this was a test by her adversary, just like Eve in the garden. She will have to make a choice. Just as she was about to open the door, her phone ranged. Who could that be this time of night? Chanel quickly and quietly tiptoed back to her bedroom to retrieve her phone. It was her friend Courtney. *This is your way out! Choose!* Chanel was stuck. She couldn't choose between the lust of her body or the way out of the hell hole. She looked down at her phone and up at the ceiling. *I'm sorry, Lord.* Chanel chose to ignore the phone call and talk with Trey instead. She raced back to the door and opened it, hoping he was still out there. Nope, he had already gone back in. Not wasting a second, Chanel knocked on Trey's door. He opened it and stared at her, blankly with sleepy eyes.

"Hey, I'm sorry, were you sleeping?"

"Yes."

"Oh, I'm sorry. I didn't mean to bother you."

"It's fine. What's up?"

"I was having a rough night and needed someone to talk to."

"Okay, hold on," as he closed his door for a second and came back out with a cigarette. He sat down on the lower level steps as Chanel sat on the upper level. He lit his cigarette,

"What's up?"

"Well, I think I figured out why I have some sort of attachment to you." Chanel started. She looked at Trey looking at her full in the face with his cigarette hanging off his bottom lip. "I have daddy issues." She scoffed. Trey chuckled to himself, "really," he said.

"Yes, really!"

"I barely knew my daddy is growing up. He was out and about doing his own thing. I would see him now and then. Sometimes he would buy me clothes and shoes. But, we didn't have a connection. We didn't have a bond. And the lack of affection I got from my dad, I kind of got that from you. I think that's why you are so comfortable with me. I enjoy your company, but I know it's because of the relationship I have with my dad." Chanel finished

"I'm sorry that happened to you. I'm sorry he wasn't there for you. You know I care about you, and I would never do anything to hurt you," Andrew said. Chanel found herself falling for him again. "Chanel," Trey said, as he caressed her leg, "I care about you. How yo daddy treated you wasn't right. He should have been there for you."

"Right," she said. Chanel sat on the steps and looked at her hands. She started thinking about her childhood. As she reminisced on the good and bad, she forgot that Trey was caressing her leg, making his way up her thigh.

"Trey, please," she said.

"What?" he said, "c'mon Chanel. Please," he begged her as he looked into her eyes. Chanel's body screamed at the temptation of him, however, her conscious knew it was wrong. She waited for the Lord to give her another sign to leave. Just one more character. But there was nothing. The Lord was quiet. The hallway was silent. The world was calm. Everyone was waiting to see what Chanel would choose. As Chanel tried to contemplate her decision, Trey made it for her. He opened Chanel's legs and licked her through her panties. She felt her body rejoice, but her mind and her heart was deeply saddened. She wanted to stop, she tried to control her body, but at this moment, she was weak and gave into her temptation. She leaned back and let Trey make love to her vagina with his tongue. She pushed his tongue deeper inside her. As he massaged inner parts with his tongue, he reached his hand up and caressed her breast through her t-shirt with one hand, and stuck his fingers in her butt with the other. Trey started pinching her nipples, and Chanel moaned out in ecstasy. Trey continued to bring her to her limit. Then he abruptly stopped. Confused, Chanel asked,

"Why you stop?"

"Follow me and see". Chanel got up and followed Trey into his apartment. He led her to his bedroom and laid her down on the bed. The house was dark. Trey rummaged around on his dresser, looking for something. The only light came from his bedroom window. As Chanel laid on Trey's bed, her thoughts guilted her. **What are you doing here? Leave? You know this man is no good for you. You know you are going against God being here. Leave.** But Chanel couldn't leave. She was ashamed. She was embarrassed. She knew Trey was no good for her. Yet, she was addicted to his tongue. It was liquid kryptonite. Finally, Trey stopped rummaging around and came to her.

"So, what is this about?" Chanel questioned,

"Well, I want to try this anal lube on you. I know you like anal sex. This lube is strawberry flavored. I was thinking after anal sex, you lick it off."

"What?" Chanel sat right up. **See, told you, you should have left. He's perverted**.

"Yea, I wanted to try this lube on you, and you lick it off. I've been thinking about what if you started oral sex on me! Don't get me wrong; I love doing you. But sometimes, I want the favor returned. Are you interested?" Chanel wasn't interested. Matter of fact, she was disgusted. She wanted to leave right then and there. Yet, she stayed because she knew Trey would throw a fit. She should have never come into his condo.

"Sure. Why not," she replied. Trey started kissing her body in the dark. He made a trail of kisses from her nipples to clit. His tongue was soft and warm as he planted wet kisses. He started licking her like a 7/11 Slurpee; he placed a condom on his penis and poured the lube all over it. He then worked his penis inside her anus. Chanel felt discomfort. She didn't like it. She started to feel weird. It felt weird. Honestly, because she considered him as demonic, she viewed the anal sex as expanding his perverted four-play. *Yuck*, her mind screamed. Chanel's body began to react to what her mind was thinking. She slowly was no longer turned on by his seduction wanted out of his room, apartment, and back into hers where she could take a cold shower. Trey, who had no clue to what

Chanel was feeling, was in for a rude awakening. Chanel finally had enough and said,

"Trey, please stop". No response. He kept going.

"Trey, please stop, seriously," as she started pushing him off her. She felt him stop but couldn't see his face. She couldn't see his body language either. It was dark. He sat between her legs for a moment and said,

"What's wrong?'

"This whole thing. I didn't come over here for this. I should have never come."

"What is that supposed to mean?'" "It means that I know better, and I dug myself into a deeper hole by being here. I know this is not pleasing to God. I'm trying hard to fight off my attraction to you. I need to stop using you as a way to escape my problems." "Stop using me?" he repeated. *Oh crap, I've said too much!*

"Just forget, I ever said anything." Chanel got up and looked for her underwear in the dark.

"What you mean using me?" he demanded.

"Nothing Trey," she said.

"Nah," he said as he got louder. "You're using me?" By then, Chanel found her underwear and hurried to the front door. Trey hurried and put his penis up and was quickly on her trial. Chanel flung the door open and ran down the steps. Trey, who was right behind her, said,

"So you've been using me? Are you serious! So all this time, you've been using me!" Chanel finally made it to her door and opened it quickly, and closing it tightly! She locked the door out of fear of Trey. Trey then started banging on her door yelling,

"'See, this that stuff I will be talking about"

'What stuff?"

"You always get what you want, but whenever I want something, you run away. That's selfish. Then I found out that you've been using me!"

"First of all, you are the one who always offered! You always take it upon yourself."

"You never stop me!" Chanel couldn't do this anymore! She realized this exchange was unhealth. She needed to free herself from Trey's grasp finally! Chanel went inside her bedroom and locked the door. She was afraid that Trey might break it down. She left him there to deal with his problems. One thing was exact; if she genuinely wanted freedom from this demon she was fighting, she will have to make a choice and stick with it.

The next morning, Chanel felt defeated. She couldn't believe that she allowed herself to go over to Trey's house yet again. Especially after everything she knew. However, she still gave into her temptation. She keeps digging this whole. She felt guilty, asking God for help, only to do the deed yet again. She felt like a bothersome child. She thought God would be so angry at her that she didn't' even want to apologize for what she had down. She thought her fate was sealed. Her phone rang, interrupting her thoughts. It was her friend Courtney.

"Hello?""Hey, girl, are you alright. I saw I missed your call?"

"Yes, I'm fine," Chanel started.

"Are you sure?" Chanel thought about it for a moment.

"No, I'm not fine. So, it happened again last night."

"What happened?"

"Me and my neighbor. After you left, I let him do that thing, he invited me back to his house, we wanted to do stuff I wasn't comfortable with, and I started to feel guilty, and now I feel like crap," Chanel said. She put her head down and cried.

"Chanel, please don't feel guilty. I do understand your frustration. However, I want you to know you are worthy. When I say worthy, I mean you are worthy of a good relationship. You are worthy of a good man. You are worthy, and you do not have to keep putting yourself in this toxic situation. You can walk away."

"How can I walk away when I keep going back, Courtney. It's like when I try to free myself; I get sucked back in."

"Well, for starters, have you asked God for help?"

"Yes, I HAVE."

"What did he say?"

"He said that I keep going around this same mountain."

"Mhm, like the Hebrews when they left Egypt."

"Huh?"

"In the bible, the Hebrews went around the same mountain for forty years. They didn't walk into the land of milk and honey because they chose not to let go of the old stuff they did in Egypt. Chanel, you have to make a choice. Do you want the land of milk and honey does you want to be stuck going around the same mountain. You are not in Egypt anymore." Chanel sat and looked at the phone. She wanted to hang up on Courtney, but she heard God say, *"listen to what she has to say."*

'Courtney, I don't know how to get out of Egypt. I feel like I'm getting stuck."

"Okay. What exactly have you been feeling, besides guilt."

"Anger."

"Towards?"

"My dad. I still blame him. Like my heart is full of rage and anger towards him. I almost want to say I hate him for the trauma he passed on to me. And I shared this with my neighbor."

"You shared what?"

"I shared with him about my dad and parents. Especially my dad."

"I see."

"You see what?"

"I can see how the past still haunts you to this very day. And in this very moment, I hear you. I hear the wounded, hurt, a confused child screaming out to me. She is hurt. She is afraid. She is confused. She is angry. She is unsure. Chanel, I want you to know that it's not your fault. None of it is. However, Chanel, I must tell you that your neighbor does not care about you. Chanel, he's using you. He took your moment of vulnerability and used it to his advantage. You have to understand that when men prey on women, they prey on a certain type of woman. Women who they consider vulnerable and weak. You open yourself up like that to him made him look at you as weak. It instantly registered that he can take advantage of you. This is why he keeps taking advantage of you. He makes you feel guilty about saying no. And I bet this somehow correlates to your rape. When you told Andrew no, and he took advantage of you. All these men, Chanel, are taking advantage of you. And disguise in a way that makes it seem beneficial to you when in reality it's only benefitting them. It's like when the bible says your adversary prowls around like a roaring lion looking for someone to devour. I think I said this to you last night and, I will repeat it. When you watch lions in the wild, Chanel, who do they go after? They go after the weak, the sick, and the old. Because they know that they are too weak to fight back and won't see the attack coming." As Courtney continued talking, Chanel finally started accepting what Courtney had to say. All this time, she was fighting her, but she decided to let Courtney in and allow Courtney's words to penetrate her heart like never before. Chanel got choked up and started crying hard. Courtney heard her friend. Instead of talking, she remained silent and gave Chanel the space needed to call.

"Courtney, I don't know if I can do this."

"Yes, you can. And I will be right here with you."

"Courtney, I don't know how to heal. It's hard."

"It's only hard because you believe it's hard. Let's start with this. Chanel, tells, yourself I love myself."

"Huh?"

"Tell yourself you love yourself?'

"That's silly."

"No, it not. Say it." Chanel was silent. She didn't want to say that. She felt silly.

"Chanel, says it," Courtney said again.

"I love myself" Chanel mumbled.

"Say it louder."

"I love myself,."

"Say it as you mean it."

"I love myself."

"Say it while laughing." Chanel started laughing.

"Say it."

"I love myself," Chanel said through small laughter.

"Say it in an angry voice."

"I love myself."

"Say it in a sad voice."

"I love myself."

"Say it in a depressed voice."

"I love myself."

"Say it in an anxious voice."

"I love myself."

"Say it in a silly voice."

"I love myself."

"Say it in a sexy voice."

"I love myself."

"Say it in a quiet voice."

"I love myself."

"Whisper it to yourself."

"I love myself."

"Now stand up." Chanel stood up on her bedroom floor.

"Now jump up and down and say I love myself." Chanel started laughing and said, "I love myself."

"Now, reach your hands to the ceiling as you jump and say you love yourself."

Chanel reached her hands to the ceiling while jumping said, "I love myself."

"Okay, now hug yourself and say it." Chanel hugged herself and said, "I love myself."

"How do you feel?' Courtney said. Chanel was quiet. She felt silly and squminsh. She also felt a bit embarrassed.

"Weird."

"Why weird?"

"I've never done that before."

"How does your heart feel?"

"My heart feels better."

"That's good. I want you to practice saying that to yourself. I want you to know that you love *you*. I truly believe that you've been putting yourself in these situations because you don't value yourself due to life circumstances. However, now is the time to take responsibility for what happened in the past in move on. It's time to heal Chanel. We can't keep going around this mountain. I won't let you." Chanel started to feel empowered.

"I also believe that this attraction to this older man is a result of unresolved daddy issues."

"You think so?"

"Yes, It's not ironic that you are attracted to this older man. He seems comforting, sweet, and kind, but he's also manipulative. He attended to your needs. There has to be a moment in your life where this type of behavior was or another behavior that your dad did that reinforced that this was okay." Courtney finished.

"Okay, well, how do I resolve my daddy issues?"

"By forgiving Chanel. I mean, really forgiving him for the hurt he caused. That is the only way you can move past this mountain. Forgiveness will set you free. Bitterness, hurt, rage, anger, guilt, and shame will leave once you forgive your dad." Chanel thought about Courtney's words. She remembered God instructed her to do this last night.

"Okay, one more question?"

"Okay."

"What if you're not ready to forgive that person?"

"Well, my question would be, what do you get by being the victim of your own story?" Chanel was quiet.

"Nothing."

"Exactly. People have a hard time moving on from pain and trauma because they like being victims of their own stories. It gives them sympathy. It gives them energy. It gives them validation for being hurt. You don't need anyone to validate your feelings because your feelings are real. However, you have to check your feelings and not allow your feelings to dictate your life. If you truly want freedom, then you have to forgive. Think of God. I know this might seem like a cliché answer, but seriously think of God. When he forgives us, he's not doing it because we deserve it, he does it because it is a reflection of his heart. It is a reflection of who he is. He forgives us freely, so he doesn't be angry at us. This forgiveness comes from his son Jesus who died for us, Chanel. He was mercy and grace. God knows human nature is corrupt. He also knows you struggle in this area. He also ready to meet you here too. Just let him in."

Chanel broke down and cried. "I want to forgive my dad. But I have so much anger in my heart."

"Okay, my advice is to write a letter to your dad. You are saying everything. Mention everything that ever happened between the two of you. After you write your letter, tell him he no longer has control over you anymore and that you are not living a life full of love and forgiveness." Chanel closed her eyes and tried to imagine what this letter would be like.

"Okay, one more question."

"Okay, what's that?"

"How do you deal with temptation?"

"What do you mean?"

"Well, I mean, how do you deal with the temptation of freeing yourself from something that you know isn't good for you?"

'Well, it depends on how you view it?'

"What you mean?"

"Well, how do you view the temptation? Do you view from a place of victimization, or do you view from a place of victory?" Chanel got silent. "Victimization"

"That's good that you admitted that. That is the first step. Secondly, you have to change your perception? First, you must understand why you view it from a place of victimization, after you understand that, after, you must train your mind to view it from a place of victory. You must view it as if you've already defeated the temptation. If you tell your mind that the temptation is hard to defeat, and it's hard to break, your mind will believe it. Now, if you tell your mind that you will beat this temptation and move forward, you will. Your mind only believes what you tell it is true. Now Chanel, do you believe why you can beat this temptation?"

Chanel was hesitated, "yes."

"No hesitation Chanel. You have to believe it truly."

With more security in her voice, Chanel answered, "yes."

"That's awesome. I also urge you to write it down. First, write down what you desire, then write down your end goal, write down anything that could potentially get in the way, and finally write down a plan to help you reach your desire. I'm sharing this with you because I think you will benefit from this."

"Okay, thank you."

"Chanel, are you committed to doing the work?"

"Yes." "Okay, I will hold you accountable. If you need help or support, just reach out to me. I will be there to help you."

"Thank you so much, Courtney I appreciate you so much."

"No problem Chanel. I love you, girl."

"I love you too. Thank you for being there for me." "No problem. What are friends for?" Both ladies hung up the phone, and for the first time, Chanel finally felt that this nightmare was about to be over. So Chanel got up and paced her apartment. She wanted the perfect to ask God for deliverance and heal her from her childhood pain. Chanel kept walking the room, hoping the ideal words would come out. Then finally, God spoke and said, *"Chanel, do not get caught up in the fancy wording. Let your heart speak. I am always listening, and I know what you need before you ask it."* After the Lord spoke, Chanel felt a sense of peace wash over her. She allowed God's peace to pulsate through her, filling her entire being,; from the top of her head to the soles of her feet,; she felt God. Then finally she said, *"Dear Heavenly Father. This has been a nightmare. But, before I get started on me, first I want to say thank you. My walk is not perfect with you, God but I'm trying. I know you ask us to try, and I know that you are strong in my weakness. I want to say thank you for being strong enough to carry someone like me. Thank you for seeing the beauty and wholeness in me when I didn't even see it within myself. Thank you for saving me from my own hands when I tried to take my life. Thank you for sealing your redemption promise by your son Jesus Christ who died on the cross for my sins. Thank you that he sacrificed his life for someone like me. Thank you for the undeserved grace and mercy that you freely give me. Thank you for your patience and gentle correcting that pushes me into your arms and the path you are steering me away from. Father, I got myself into this pickle. For so long God, I've been angry at my Father. As a matter of fact, I didn't know I was mad with my father. I've been in holding in so much. My mom too. I've been angry with them for years. In addition to that, Lord, this whole rape thing with Andrew. That rape took a massive chunk out of me. It's played a massive role in the decisions I've been making thus far. That and my dad. I've been operating on a low-frequency Lord. These men that I've been dealing with are taking advantage of me. I've been allowing my situations to dictate my life when I don't have to. I've been allowing hurt and pain to rule me.*

When that rape happened, Lord it took my voice. I made it mean that my voice wasn't valuable. That my demands, wants, or wishes didn't matter that I had to follow through with what they wanted. What if I said no, that I am the bad guy. When in reality, they were manipulative and abusive. However, I see now, Lord. I can see clearly that they were no good for me. I can also see that what has happened in my past does not define me. I now see that my works do not represent my worth. I know that I am worthy, regardless of my history. That I deserve better treatment, and I do not have to succumb to the demands of a manipulative man who does not care about me. I'm learning that you care about me. I see that you have my best interest at heart. I'm seeing that you are tugging at my heart to rid this pain, hurt, bitterness, and replace it with love, forgiveness, love, and integrity. Father, please, pretty please, remove this stronghold of my life and restore in Lord. Show me what I need to do. I am at your mercy. In Jesus's name, Amen.

As the tears fell, she dropped to her knees and bowed her head in complete reverence to God. The truth is, Chanel was tired, honey. She desperately wanted a way out. After several minutes of silence, she heard the words, *"you are not guilty of any crime", "you are forgiven",* and *"you are free."* Chanel couldn't believe the words God spoke to her. She was in total awe and shock. All she could do was cry. Then God spoke again and said, *"write".* Chanel instantly knew what he was referring to the letter. It was time to free herself from this prison. So she got up and grabbed her pen and a piece of paper and titled her letter.

To the man, I wish I knew,

Dear daddy,

Should I even call you, daddy? I mean, after all, I barely saw you. I looked to you to be the one that would comfort me. The one who would be my knight in shining armor. The one who would kiss the tears away and be my protector. You were supposed to show me how a man is supposed to love a woman. You were supposed to show me how a man is to treat a woman. You were supposed to show me how a man is supposed to be. But, instead, I was met with constant let down and regret.

Do you remember the day you were supposed to show up and take me for ice cream? Remember how I waited all day on that porch for you, and you never came. My momma told me to go inside that you weren't coming. I swore for whatever reason; it was her fault you didn't show up. I remember you two had gotten into an argument the day before. I thought you were so mad at her that you didn't show up to see me. I was angry at her. I blamed her.

Or do you remember how you skipped my high school graduation? You said you were coming. But instead, you, of course you didn't show. You didn't show up for me. You claimed my mother never gave you a ticket. When in reality, she did. I found out that you were "on the block.".

How come the block always came before me? How come you didn't care about me enough to see how I was doing? How come I wasn't your top priority?

Do you remember when you went to jail and all of sudden you wanted to see me? You would write to me, and I would tear your letters to shreds. No, you don't get to pick me up when you want to. When I needed you most, you never showed up. You weren't there.

You weren't there when momma and I lived in poverty. You weren't there when she kicked me out. You weren't there when I got raped by that boy. I wanted you to protect me!

I wanted to have an excellent relationship with you. I use to daydream about us running away together, starting a new life. I would envision you getting a good job and getting on your feet. I would go on to graduate college, get married, and have children. Your grandchildren would love you. You would have been the world's most loved grandfather.

I had a burning desire for you to be the one I could depend on for everything. I see now that I put my hope in you when I should have been putting my hope in God.

You know, I never held you accountable. I mean I never really did. I blamed my mother for everything. It even trickled into my adult life and relationships with me. I typically end up giving them sympathy when they are the ones who are hurting me, just like you. I gave you so much sympathy when you were the one who was hurting me. You were the one who put the dagger in my heart. Now I'm bleeding.

However, now I am removing the blade that you left, and by the power of God, he is healing the wound that you left. Christ, Jesus! Finally healed me!

Thank you, God for the healing.

But now, daddy, with all the pain you have caused me, I need to do one more thing. And that is forgiving you. That's right, daddy I forgive you. God is showing me that by human error we are bound to make mistakes. Daddy, I forgive you for not showing up. Daddy, I forgive you for your lies and deceit. I forgive you for the hurt you caused me. I forgive you for the pain. I realize now that holding on to this pain is only hurting me. That me holding on to the hurt will never solve anything. It prolongs the process. I will not hold my process up anymore. I will move forward in my healing and let go of any pain or hurt you have caused. Daddy, not only do I forgive you, daddy, I love you. Yes, I love you. God commands me to love you. Daddy, I release any pain in my heart that resides. I am a free woman.

I want to thank you, I want to thank you for giving me my first heartbreak. But God is building my heart back, and it will be anew. I love you, daddy so much that I release this thing I've been holding onto for me! And when it's all said

and done, I know that I will see you again in the afterlife by faith. And the slate between us will be clean.
　Sincerely,
　Your amazing, strong, beautiful daughter,
　Chanel Elaine Johnson.

After Chanel finished writing her letter, she felt an immediate shift in her body. A weight was lifted off her chest. The peace of God still resided in her, and for the first time, she felt whole and complete, lacking in nothing.

New Beginnings

A younger Chanel was playing on her porch with a neighbor. They were making mud pies. Chanel was having the time of her life in imagination play. Then her neighbor tapped her shoulder, "that man in the car is looking at you." Chanel looked from her playing to find indeed a man looking at her from his car. He was smiling. She was perplexed and scared because she didn't know why this man was smiling at her. She kept looking and looking, trying to figure out who it was. Then suddenly it clicked, "Daddy!!!!" she screamed as she ran full speed off the steps. She ran right up to the car.

"Hi, daddy! I missed you so much; where have you been?" It's been months since Chanel saw her dad. She wasn't always sure why she didn't see him, but she just rolled with it.

"Hey, baby. How are you?" he asked. Chanel was super excited to see him but also nervous. She didn't want her mother to come out and see that her daddy was there. She knew they didn't get along.

"What you looking all scared for. Get in?" Chanel was hesitant. She didn't want to upset her mother, but she wanted to be with her dad. She didn't know who to be loyal too.

"I don't want my mommy to be upset. Maybe I should go ask her."

"I'm yo, daddy. You ain't gotta ask yo momma permission to get in my car. I made you!" Chanel's father said in a stern tone. Chanel was scared. So, Chanel got in the car. She was a bit nervous. She hadn't seen her dad in almost like forever. It felt weird being with him. She sat in the passenger seat, unsure what to do or say.

"Give me a hug!" he said excitedly. He reached over and gave Chanel the biggest, warmest hug. Chanel, only eight years old at the time, was anxious. She couldn't take her mind off, disappointing her mother, but she wanted her dad too. She hugged him back.

"So, what's up. You alright?"

"Yes."

"Alright. You need some money?" Chanel just looked at him. She wasn't sure what to say.

"Uhm, I guess so." "Ain't no guess so. Do you need some money? A closed mouth doesn't get fed."

"Yes," she said. Her dad handed her $5.

"Thank you."

"So, are you straight?"

"Yes?"

"You sure? Me and your uncle about to ride to the store. You want something?"

"Yes, some chips and a soda."

"Aight, I'll be back." Chanel got out of the car, and her uncle got in the passenger seat. The two men road away to the store. Chanel went back to playing with her friend, who was watching on the porch.

"Was that your daddy?"

"Yes."

"Dang, that's tight. His car tight too." "I know. He's so tight." Chanel giggled. She enjoyed talking about her dad with her neighbor. Them her daddy pulled back up with the snacks. Chanel once again ran full speed down the steps. She was happy to have a bag of chips and soda. It meant a lot to her. She could remember when she would ask her mom to buy her a bag of chips and a soda and always tell her no. With her daddy, she didn't have that problem. Chanel's dad opened the door, and she got in. She opened her chips and soda.

"What do you say?"

"Thank you," she said as she smiled. Chanel dug into those chips like it was nothing. She ate those chips like she hasn't eaten in days. Her dad watched her silently as she ate her chips.

"Can we go to grandma's house?" It's been a long time since Chanel saw her grandmother. All she could remember was that her mom and dad didn't get along, and she couldn't see them for a while.

"Sure," he said. He started the car and drove to his mother's house. It wasn't far where Chanel lived with her mom. Within a few minutes, they were there. Chanel opened the car door and ran full speed up the steps. She ranged the doorbell. A feeling of nostalgia began to wash over Chanel. She could remember all the fun times she had, all the snacks, the cuddles, the love.

"Well, hello," her grandmother said as she opened the door. She greeted Chanel with a smile, and Chanel smiled back. She was super happy to see her.

"Hi grandma, I missed you so much."

"I missed you too, honey." She gave her grandma a big hug. Chanel then walked herself into the house and began to remember what it felt like to be there. She familiarized herself with every room. In the kitchen, she asked,

"Grandma, you got any snacks?"

"Yes, baby. What would you like?"

"Some cookies. Is grandpa here?"

"Why yes, he is. He's in the bedroom. You remember how to get there, don't you?"

"Yes, ma'am." Chanel made her way to her grandparent's room. Her grandfather was putting his watch on the dresser.

"Hey, grandpa!" Chanel yelled with excitement. Her grandfather turned around and said, *"Chanel, is that you? Get on over here and give me a hug, girl!"* Chanel was so happy to see him. He was warm and loving. She ran over and embraced her grandfather. He gave her the biggest hug.

"How have you been? It's been a while since I've laid my eyes on you."

"I'm doing well, grandpa. I missed you so much."

"How is school?"

"School is fun! I'm learning all types of cool stuff." "Oh yea?"" "Dinosaurs, stars, comets, everything."

"Yea, that sounds like fun. You need some money?"

"Uhm, I think I'm okay. My dad gave me some money."

"Oh, he did. Well, I'm going to give you some more." Chanel's granddad gave her another $5.

"Thanks, grandpa," Chanel said excitedly.

"Chanel," her grandma called.

"Yes?" She answered back as she made her way back to the kitchen. Her grandmother had packed her a snack bag.

"Thanks, grandma." Chanel was very excited.

"Chanel," her dad called, "it's time to go." Chanel was sad. She just got there. She wasn't ready to leave. She wanted to stay. It's been so long that since she's seen them. She wished she could stay with them forever. It wasn't fair. She barely gets to see them. She has to stay with her mean mommy. Chanel sulked as she walked towards the front door. She found her dad standing there waiting on her. She said goodbye to both of her grandparents and walked to her dad's car. He waved goodbye to his parents and got in the driver's seat.

"Cheer up. You'll see them again," he said as she started the car. Chanel just put her head down and twiddled her thumbs. Her dad drove her back home. Within a few minutes, Chanel was ago at home. Then she suddenly remembered that her mom was still in the house sleeping. She hoped she didn't wake up and saw that Chanel had left. She didn't want to be in trouble. Her dad reached over and said,

"Chanel, I love you."

"Okay," Chanel responded . She didn't know how to express her emotions. It felt weird to her. This was uncommon for her to say those words. She didn't say them often.

"You hear me; I love you, Chanel. I know things are sticky right now. But I love you, Chanel. Your daddy is trying to get his stuff together. I want you to know that you mean a lot to me. I will always love you, no matter what. Daddy is going to get his stuff together and come and get you." Chanel believed him. She hoped for the day her daddy

would come for her. Chanel hugged her daddy back, "I love you too, daddy" she said before. Then she got out of the car and watched her daddy pull away. Then a stiff feeling in her throat sunk into her stomach. She felt heavy, sad, and confused. She wanted her dad, and she couldn't understand why she couldn't have him.

Chanel made an appointment with her old counselor. She told them that she needed to see her ASAP because she needed help navigating through a challenging situation. After many attempts and back and forth with the receptionist, Chanel finally landed an appointment for 1:30. Chanel arrived at the building around 1:15 pm. She hurriedly walked inside and waited to be called. Chanel was too nervous because it had been so long since she's seen her psychologist. Chanel waited in the cold waiting room, anticipating for her name to be called. Chanel psychologist walked into the waiting room and found Chanel sitting down reading a magazine.

"Hello, Chanel, how are you?" her psychologist asked.

"I'm doing okay, yourself?" Chanel asked as she stood from her seat.

"I'm doing great. It's been a while since I've last seen you. I'm glad we can talk again," her psychologist said as she escorted Chanel to the back room. Chanel followed closely behind. She wondered what she would say. How will she talk about everything? Will she need to come back for another visit? They finally made it to the room, and the psychologist motioned her to sit on the couch. Chanel took her seat and waited for her psychologist to sit down across from her. Once she took her seat, she asked,

"So, how has everything been going?"

"Things have been okay."

"Just okay?"

"Uhm, in the middle. It's hard to explain it honestly."

"Take your time."

"Well, I got involved with this man."

"Oh, dating again?"

"Well, not exactly that."

"Mhm," she said, keeping her face in a neutral tone.

"Uhm, it all started when I moved into this apartment. My neighbor, who lives above me, would see me occasionally. I used to avoid him. I was a bit nervous about having a conversation. So one day, he told me I was unapproachable and standoffish. I didn't understand why he would say that. So I changed my demeanor to appear more friendly. He claimed he wanted to get to know me and be "friends." I was a little unsure about that because I barely knew him, but he seemed nice. So I went ahead and "befriended" him. We would talk, and the conversation would be good. We would go over the each-others house, share food, all of those things. Then one day, he asked if I would spend the night, and I declined. He wanted to feel a woman's body. So then from their, it escalated to hugs. But his hugs were different. They seemed sexual in nature. He would feel on me in the process. I didn't like that. Then he would make me feel guilty for not giving him what he wanted. I didn't like that either. So, I would avoid talking to him for some days. Then one day, he followed me to school. I felt super uncomfortable with him doing that. He claimed because he wanted to apologize for how he was acting. But still, I didn't feel comfortable with him following me to school. And I'm not sure how it happened, but we can sexual with each other. I think the first time was when he knocked on my door. I had on only a robe because I was in the shower. He wanted to apologize about something, and as usual, he wanted a hug. I gave in I hugged him because I didn't want to hear his mouth. Then he started feeling and touching all over me, which led to kissing; the kissing led to discovering I was naked under the robe; he then led me to my bedroom and performed oral sex on me. I felt a little weird. Because he kind of just, you know did it. I was baffled. I didn't know what to do. So I complied. It was like my conscience was saying no, but my body was telling yes. Then, now I'm in this pickle. Where he performs oral sex on me, and I don't always want it. But he makes me feel guilty if I don't give him what he wants, whether that is him performing oral sex on me, him giving me a hug, him wanting to try different sexual things on me. I've done anal with this man, and I feel dirty. I feel used. I feel like no one will ever want me.

Then all these problems are coming up about my dad. The relationship I had with him, how he was never in my life that much, how my problems are stemming from daddy issues, how I am afraid to stick to my boundaries because I afraid of upsetting them, how I let men do what they want with me, then the rape and how that affected me. I even reached out to my rapist, and I told him how he's responsible for what he's done to me, and I'm just confused."

Chanel was crying as she spoke. She grabbed some tissue and wiped away her tears. She held herself and rocked back and forth.

Her psychologist was quiet. She studied Chanel with a neutral glance.

"Well, it seems like you've been going through a lot; some manipulation, some resentment, some forgiveness issues, some bitterness, some low self-value moments. I want to address each piece of this puzzle. That will require you to come back for another session. Is that something you are okay with doing?"

"Yes," Chanel responded through her tears.

"Oka is good. The first thing I want to speak about is how you're viewing yourself during this process. Chanel, do you value yourself?" Chanel was silent. She couldn't speak. All she could do was cry.

"Chanel, it appears that a lot of what is happening is because of how you view yourself -not excusing your neighboring being manipulative. Because what he is doing is wrong. But I want to talk about you. I want to get to the core of the issue. I believe the answer lies in you. You are the one you are looking for. I listened to the story about your rape and your anger towards your father, which we will address; however, I believe this is Chanel's pattern. This pattern is buried deep in your subconscious and could have been developed by the broken relationship with you dad. I think you are unknowingly putting yourselves in similar situations over and over again. Like with the rapist, he has some of the same characteristics as your neighbor. Manipulative, controlling, makes you feel guilty for not giving in to his demands, you not standing up for yourself, you giving in to what they want, then you going home hating yourself more. You leaving that situation just to find yourself in another very similar. Chanel, I know

I'm a psychologist, and I'm not supposed to talk about God, but I need to tell you something. Chanel, what you are going through is a soul-tie. Soul-ties are deadly. It can keep you in the same cycle. It keeps you bound. You read your bible. Remember that story about the woman with the issue of blood?

"Yes," Chanel answered.

"Do you remember how long she dealt with it?"

"No, not exactly." "For twelve years. For twelve years, she had an issue with blood. I'm pretty sure they tried everything on her in those twelve years. So she suffered because we can assume no one could help her. Then one day when, Jesus was on his to bring back to life a twelve-year-old girl. She saw Jesus, reached out, and touched his robe. Now we know that the woman was healed because of her faith. However, I want to bring to your attention the period. That woman suffered twelve years. Just like you, she carried around this burden on her back for a long time. Nothing seemed to help her. Then one day, she crawled and was touched by the faith and was healed like you, Chanel. I believe you are here because of your faith and because you are ready to heal.

To do that, we must open up about some things. Chanel, I want you to think about how you felt about your dad? I want you to close your eyes and sit quietly with yourself and travel back to your childhood. I want you to think and be intentional about it. What feelings come up when you feel about your dad?" Chanel, who sat quietly listening to her psychologist, closed her eyes and started to replay her childhood. She remembers her dad, how he was in and out, how she wanted him to be there so bad, how she didn't always see him, why he never saw her often if he cared about her, did she matter to him.

"What do you see?"

"I see me wanting my dad. I see him being in and out. I see him not always see me. I see him only giving me money here and there. I see him not being involved with me."

"Okay, did that make you feel at that age?" "It made me feel sad. I wanted to be with my dad. I wanted his love. I wanted him around. I wanted his approval."

"What do you mean by approval?"

"I mean, I that with him, I didn't feel like I was good enough." When the words left Chanel's lips, she froze. Then all of a sudden, the memories surged. She saw instances of her wanting approval by her father, her wanting him to congratulate her on her success but he was never there, her coming home with A's and B's, but her mother would scorn her for the B's. They could be better, how she was forced to be perfect all the time, how she would perform for others approval and validation because the little girl inside of her felt rejected. Her father's lack of participation in her life left her feeling rejected and not good enough. Chanel didn't realize that she was crying hysterically. Her psychologist kept calling her name. "Chanel, Chanel," she said in an urgent tone.

"Yes," Chanel finally spoke in tears.

"Talk to me; how are you feeling?"

"I feel the pain of the little girl. I see a little me wanting her dad and wanting anting him in her life and wondering why she could never have him? Why was he always so distant? Why didn't he care about me? I see the broken little girl."

"Chanel, open your eyes," her psychologist instructed. Chanel opened her eyes.

"Chanel, you don't have to be the broken little girl anymore. The broken little girl needs healing so that older Chanel can move on with her life. So that older Chanel can stop putting other's needs before hers. So that older Chanel can stop performing for other benefits. So older Chanel can no longer feel guilty about setting boundaries. So that older Chanel can now take control of her life. So that older Chanel can forgive her father and let God restore the peace that has been robbed of you." Chanel was stunned. She sat in silence across from her psychologist.

"Chanel, how old are you?"

"I'm 19.'

"How old were you when your father first hurt you that you can remember?" "I was about 8 or 9 years old." "Okay, for so ten years of your life, you have been carrying this pain. You've been carrying this load, yes?" "Yes." "10 years is a long time to hold on to pain, hurt, and trauma. Chanel, are you ready to let it go? Are you ready to forgive yourself? Are you ready to forgive your father? Are you ready to let older Chanel make the decisions?"

"Yes." "Good, so I want you to commit to saying one thing to yourself every morning, every night, every day, every afternoon, all the time when you are feeling low. Are you ready?"

"Yes." "Okay, I want you to say to yourself, I love myself," Chanel remembers when her friend Courtney instructed her to do this.

"Say it." "I love myself." "Repeat it."

"I love myself."

"Say it louder."

"I love myself." "Say it louder." "I love myself," Chanel yelled. She giggled. The weight on her chest started to fall off.

"Okay, Chanel, I want you to say that to yourself every single day. Understand."

"Yes."

I want to commit to measuring your mood over the next week or so until we come back. I want you to write down everything you are feeling. Sad. Happy. Mad. Confused. I want you to start journaling your emotions. It's not good to keep them locked inside. Pick a anytime of the day to write in your journal. Writing is a good way to release unwanted emotions. It may also do you well to read over your words. Sometimes the answer to a lot of our problems reveal themselves in many ways. Reading your own words can be a great way to understanding ourselves and why we views things the way we do. Also, I want you to get in the habit of saying a favorite affirmation or bible scripture when you are down. Write them down in a journal or sticky note and post them around. Reading an affirmation or bible scripture in your own handwriting is a wonderful tool to remind yourself you are worthy. I want you to be intentional about the environment you're creating. You can also invite a friend to help stay on track and be accountable. Are you willing to do this?

"Yes."

"Good. I think Chanel, that once you start journaling about your day, telling yourself that you love yourself, and posting reading words of affirmations, you will be free from your neighbor's manipulation and create the healthy boundaries, you need. I just want you to know that you do not have to please him. You do not have to perform for him. If he gets upset about your boundaries that doesn't make you a bad person, okay."

"Okay."

"I'm glad you are taking control of your life. This is wonderful. I want to schedule another appointment with you. When are you available next. I can clear my schedule or plug you in on any day."

"Is it okay if I come back next week?" "Absolutely. What day. September 14th."

"Okay, next Friday. What time?"

"Same time."

"Okay, 1:30 it is. I will see you next week Chanel. I look forward to your progress." "Thank you." Chanel got up from her seat and walked towards the door. Her psychologist walked behind her. Chanel was quiet. She replayed everything her psychologist said.

"Don't think too hard on it. Let the words flow from you." "Okay."

"You have any plans today?" "No"

"You should go hang out with some friends. Enjoy the sun and have some fun, especially after a session like this. You opened up and released a lot of emotional baggage and trauma. You need to do something fun and uplifting." "Okay," Chanel said as she made it to the door. Chanel waved her psychologist by and headed to her car.

Inside her car, Chanel texted her friend Courtney.

"Hey girl, I just left my psychologist's office."

"Oh word, how did it go?"

"I went well. She taught me a lot. Plus, she also mentioned WOOP to me too. So, you know, that means I have to do it. I have to come back next week and report my progress with it." "Oh, really,. That's what's up."

"Also, at the advice of my therapist, she wanted me to reach out to a friend and go have some fun. I did lots of crying today, and she wanted to help take my mind of this stuff. Are you free?"

"I will be in a few minutes. I can come over, and we can watch movies."

"Awesome! Red box and pizza!"

"It' s a date." Chanel felt super excited. She started the car and begun the drive home. She was happy knowing that she was making a turn in the right direction. She did want freedom from Trey, Andrew, her dad, the rape, not feeling good enough. She needed a fresh start, a new beginning. It meant so much to her that her life was changing for the better. She knew that she was making a step in the right direction. As she drove, her thoughts shifted to Trey. She wondered how he would react. All she could do was pray for the best and stick to her boundaries. Chanel stopped by the Walgreens by her house and went to the red box. She picked out a fun movie to watch with her friend. *"We can order pizza and wings when she gets there."* Chanel paid for the movie and got back into her car. She rounded the corner and pulled into the gated community. She pulled into the gate and headed towards her condo. The sun was shining, and the felt terrific outside. Chanel took a deep breath and breathed in the cold crisp air letting it fill her lungs. She walked into the building and headed towards her door. Her thoughts so occupied Chanel that she didn't notice

Trey standing on the steps looking at her. "Hey, Chanel." Chanel looked up startled. Her heart started beating fast. She begun to silently panic. *What do I do, what do I do, what do I do? "Relax,"* the holy spirit said to her.

"Hey Trey," she said as she tried to gain her composure.

"I haven't seen you in a few days. Everything good?" "Yes, everything is fine. Thank you."

"Aw, okay. How are you today? You look very lovely."

"I'm doing well, and thank you." "You smell good too."

"Thank you. I appreciate that as well."

"mhm," he said as he licked his lips. Chanel closed her eyes and prayed to God silently. Trey came down the steps and moved closer to her.

"Can I have a hug? I just want to make sure everything is all good between us. Plus, I could use it. I'm having a rough day today." "Uhm, I don't think that's appropriate."

'What you mean you don't think that's appropriate. It's just a hug." 'To you it's just a hug, but I don't like giving you hugs, and I would really appreciate it if you didn't go back and forth with me over this."

"Back and forth. Chanel, all I'm asking for is a hug. You make it sound like I want something extra. So I can't get hugs now?"

"Trey, please don't take it personally. I just don't find it appropriate. Can you please leave it alone?"

"Aw, okay, I see how you finna act. It's like I can't get a hug. I'm not going to go overboard, I promise." 'Trey, please. I just really don't want to hug you."

"Really, Chanel?"

"Trey…" **"She said she didn't want to hug you. No, can you please excuse yourself away from my**

friend?" Chanel turned around and found her friend Courtney standing there. Courtney looked pissed. At the same time, Chanel was relieved to see her friend there.

"Oh, my bad," Trey said as he backed away. "Oh, so this you now?"

He asked.

"What does that mean?" "You know what I mean?"

"Stop entertaining him, Chanel. He's just trying to get into your head and as for you, how about you back away from my friend now!!! She doesn't have to explain anything to you. You are not her man. You are her neighbor. Leave her alone! She owes you nothing. Respect her and her wished and go on about yo business!!" Courtney said in a stern tone. Trey's face twisted into an evil stare. He looked Chanel in the eyes as he walked back up the steps. Courtney quickly opened Chanel's door and pushed her inside, followed by her. She hurriedly locked the door behind them.

"Chanel, that man is an evil spirit. Did you see the way he looked at you?" Chanel shook her head, yes.

"Chanel, I don't think it's safe for you to be here with this man lurking around her. He seems off. I think you should pack some clothes and come to my apartment until you find somewhere else to stay."

"I can just break my lease like that?"

"Well, Chanel, it's not safe for you to be here. That man is dangerous, and he showed that he doesn't care about your boundaries. He only cares about what he wants at your expense. I don't even feel safe watching a movie here. Let's come back to my dorm, and we will figure something out."

'Okay, Chanel," said. She grabbed her bookbag and packed an outfit. "Oh no, you need to stay with me for about a week."

"Are you sure?" "I'm positive." So Chanel started packing clothes for about a week's worth. She grabbed her computer, toothbrush, hair accessories, phone charger, deodorant, Bible, and journal. Once Chanel was packed and ready to go, Courtney opened Chanel's door to make sure Trey wasn't lurking around. Then she motioned for Chanel to come out. Chanel quickly locked her door and proceeded out of the building. Both ladies walked to their separate cars and headed towards Courtney's campus apartment. Courtney was a TA for the dorms she lived in. Courtney went further away from Chanel. Once the ladies made it to Courtney's dorm, they quickly went inside.

"Yea girl, I don't want you there with him anymore. He's toxic." "Well, Courtney, I appreciate you doing a thing for me." "Chanel, we are sisters for life. I've known you since preschool. I will not stand by and let him hurt you. I'm glad God allowed me to be there when he did. I can see how easy it is for you to fall into his trap. Which is why we need to get you somewhere else to live." "Okay, Courtney, what if they say no?"

"You can live here with me." "I don't know about that, Courtney." "Don't worry about it. Let's worry about it tomorrow. Tonight let's watch the movie and relax." Both ladies relaxed for the rest of the day watching movies, eating pizza and hot wings until they fell asleep.

The next morning Chanel awakened around 9 am. Courtney was still sleep. She got up and took a shower. Then she heard the bathroom door open,

"Hey, I'm about to go get some breakfast from the student store. I realize I didn't go shopping. I'm bringing back cereal and milk. Did you want anything besides that?"

"Nah, I'm good." "Okay, be back in a few." Chanel listened as Courtney shut the door. She continued her shower. She let the warm water massage her neck and shoulders. It felt nice. After washing her body, she exited the shower and put on a t-shirt and some biker shorts. She was sitting on Courtney's bean bag chair emailing her professor about makeup work to fix her grade when Courtney returned.

"Hey, girl."

"Hey… thanks for taking up for me yesterday. I appreciate that so much." 'Oh, no problem. That's what friends are for. I got your back. You got mine. What are you doing now?" "Right now, I'm emailing my professor." "Oh, okay. I was thinking, do you know if your condo building owns other properties? "Not that I know of."

"Well, after you finish doing what you are doing, we can look online and see. I was thinking maybe if they can transfer you."

"You think they would do that?' "It's possible. Anything is possible."

"Okay," Chanel said as she finished writing the email to her professor. Her grades in some of her classes were getting better. She started back studying as she once used to and did lots of extra credit work. Thank God her professors were understanding and friendly. After Chanel finished both her emails and bowl of cereal, she started to research who was in over her condominiums. She came across a few numbers online and made phone calls. No answer. She even sent an email. No answer.

"Relax, it's Saturday. I'm sure someone will get back to you. If not today, Monday." Chanel shrugged her shoulders and laid back on the bean bag chair.

"Are you okay?" Courtney asked.

"I am a little bit. I'm still trying to figure out how all of this will work in my favor."

"Believe it by faith, it will, Chanel. God knows your situation. Don't fret. God will turn it around. Believe him at his word."

"You're right."

"Yea, wanna go down and do miniature gold today?"

"Maybe, I need to do my WOOP." "Oh yea, I forgot about that. I can help you with it." "Thanks."

"No problem, let's start with your wish. What is your wish. Be intentional about this." Chanel sat and thought about the wish she most desired.

"Honoring my boundaries." "Mhm, that's a good wish. I believe you can do that." "Okay, outcomes. What are the outcomes by achieving this Wish?"

"Increased confidence, increased self-esteem, the increased value of self, increased courage, increased respect for self. It also makes me feel happy knowing that I am taking the necessary steps to treat myself like I matter. It also makes me happy that I'm breaking free of that bondage and trauma from so many years ago."

"That's amazing Chanel! I'm so happy you are breaking free of that bondage. Yes, it can keep you living in the past and it prohibits us from moving forward. I'm seeing so much growth in you. Okay, now think about what can potentially get in the way of you accomplishing your goals?" "The obstacles that can get in the way are people making me feel bad, feeling guilty for not giving them what they want, being manipulated, and feeling discouraged.

"Excellent. Now think of a Plan that will help you reach your goal."

"A plan that will help me reach my goal is using visual representation on my walls like a sticky note reminding me to honor and trust myself, distancing myself from people who do not honor my boundaries, and on the times we do cross paths remind myself that my boundaries are important, that I matter, and it's okay if people disagree with my boundaries, and I do not have change my beliefs to make them feel comfortable."

"Wow, that's good. I think that is pretty good." "Yea, it's time I stood up for me and realize that I am enough. Because I love me." Chanel said as a tear left her eye. Her friend Courtney reached out and comforted her. The two embraced each other, and Chanel felt another weight lift off her chest. Chanel pulled back, "do you think they will honestly help me find another place to stay?" "They are going to have too!"

"Well, where do we go?" "What all did you find online?"

"I found the main headquarters is this place in California." Courtney huffed.

"It has to be a local operations here." Chanel scratched her head. She pulled her laptop up again and started searching. Courtney, too, pulled out her computer and joined in on the help. Both ladies searched endlessly, looking for a local office. Then Courtney found a website that said a regional office of operations was in the county. It was about 30-45 mins away, in a county called Lakeshire.

"Okay, well, let's drive up here and see what they say. All they can say is no." Chanel felt sick.

On the car ride there, Chanel just looked out of the window. She didn't say anything. She didn't feel anything either. She just looked out the window, unsure of how everything will play out. Courtney reached over and touched Chanel's leg. Chanel looked over at Courtney. She gave a small smile -one of those smiles that don't take a lot of effort. Chanel looked back out the window. Life was changing as she knew it. She wondered what the people would say. If anyone would be there, I mean, it's a Saturday. Those office type people are usually at home out playing golf or something. The car ride to the business was quiet. Chanel closed her eyes and leaned against the glass. Before she knew it, she dozed off. When she opened her eyes again, it was Courtney tapping her shoulder. They were here. Chanel wiped the crust out of her sight and sat up straight. Her heart started beating fast. She searched the parking lot to see if there were any cars. The parking lot was empty. Chanel sunk in her seat even more.

"Don't worry, Chanel. Believe Chanel. Believe." Chanel was having trouble believing because she didn't see anyone on the lot. There was a single car there, besides there. She wasn't sure. Courtney and Chanel exited the vehicle and walked towards the building. Courtney reached out and held Chanel's hand as they walked closer to the building. Just then, this older man came out with a briefcase.

"Hello, sir. Can you please help us?" Courtney asked.

"Oh, I'm sorry. The office is closed, and I'm on my way home."

"Please, sir. My friend needs assistance." "I'm sorry I can't help. The office is closed, and I'm off the clock." He walked towards his car. Chanel felt as if all hope was lost. Then she heard a voice in her head say, *"faith"*. She thought about it, then she opened her mouth, "Excuse me, sir. I know you are on your way home, and the office is closed. But I could use some help. I'm needing help moving to a new condo or apartment building. There's a man who is manipulating me, and it's not safe for me to be there anymore if you could, please help us and point us in the right direction or something. Please." The man eyed Chanel. He squinted his eyes to study her. "I'm sorry. I wish I could help. But I have to go" as he got into his car. Chanel and Courtney just watched as the man started his car and drove off the lot. Chanel felt a hard thump form in her throat and fall into the pit of her stomach.

"Well, there goes our only hope," she thought. Chanel hugged herself and just breathed. Courtney, still determined, "don't let this get to you, Chanel, God will make away. Just believe and have faith. This is not the end." Chanel gave Courtney that same smile she gave her in the car. *"God, I need you. What do I do? You said to have faith. But the man left."* Just as Chanel finished her statement, a car drove up. It was the same car that just drove off. The man exited the car and said, "I couldn't help but notice that you look to be the same age as my daughter. And I kept telling myself, what if you were my daughter asking for help. I would want someone to help her. I'm sorry I didn't seem to care at first. I do, it just that I had to make an important meeting. But then I got this phone call saying that the meeting was canceled and then I thought about

you. I'm here to help. Please come inside." Chanel felt the tears roll down her face. Courtney and Chanel walked into the building with the man and followed him to his office. It turns out, he was over the local operations of all the condos and apartments in the state. Go figure. Once inside the man's office, Chanel told the man everything. She told him about the neighbor, her battles with acceptance, forgiveness, her father, the rape, her therapist, everything. The man's eyes widened. I'm pretty sure he didn't realize what he was getting himself into. After Chanel told her story, the man was quiet. He just stared at her for what seemed like forever, but in reality, more like five minutes.

"Well, that was a lot. I don't even know what to say. First off, I want to say I'm sorry. As a man, I'm sorry. I'm sorry that you went through that. I'm sorry about the rape. I'm sorry about the manipulation. I'm sorry about how your father treated you. You didn't deserve it. As a father myself, I know the importance of a "real father figure" and how it affects us. Fathers serve an essential role in every child's life. We teach our sons how to be men, and teach our daughters how a man is supposed to love. I want to help you. I do, and I will. I will do whatever in my power to help you. So, please leave your name and number, and I will get back to you. I promise, okay." Chanel smiled and wiped the tears from her eyes. She looked over at Courtney, who was crying too. She was grateful to have a friend like Courtney. Chanel wrote down her name and number. As she turned to leave the man got up and called to her, "Chanel," he said. She turned, and the man was getting up from his desk. "is it okay that I hug you?" Chanel said, "sure." The man reached out and gave her the biggest hug. "I felt like you needed a hug. And not one of that sexual implicit hug. Just a hug to someone who needs it. Also, P.S. I mean never let a man manipulate you to do anything. A man like that is a low operating man. He only cares for himself, as a father to a daughter. You are valuable. You are enough, and don't have to give yourself to anyone if you do not feel comfortable or ready. A man who truly cares about you will never manipulate you or make you feel guilty about what you feel is best. That is not a man; that is a boy. And your friend Courtney; she's a good friend. She cares about you. You keep her around." Chanel smiled. The man let go of his embrace while Chanel and Courtney walked out of his office.

"See, I told you, Chanel. I told you. See. I told you. Keep the faith." Chanel smiled. *"thank you, God. I am enough."*

———————————— One Week Later ————————————

Chanel hurried to her apartment to grab some clothes from her condo before heading to her therapist appointment. She was running late. She's been living with Courtney for about a week. It's been a real lifesaver. Courtney has been helping her with her journaling, helping her catch up on school work, and reminding her to repeat her mantra "I love myself" every day. She hasn't received a word from the man yet. Courtney told her to *keep the faith and wait. It will happen.* So Chanel tried her best not to worry about it. Chanel pulled into the parking lot of her condo. As usual, no one was outside. She walked towards the building and entered it. As she walked in, she ran into Trey. Chanel felt her heart stop. Her eyes got wide. He, on the other hand, just stared at her silently. Chanel tried to walk past him, but he was in the way.

"Excuse me," she said, trying to be polite. Trey ignored her.

"So, I see you ain't got your bodyguard with you. I'm surprised you came back. I didn't know you were into women. You should have told me." Chanel ignored him. She tried again to move past him. No success.

"So, are you going to ignore me, Chanel. After everything, we've been through. I thought we were better than that. You were my friend."

"Friends don't manipulate other friends." **"Manipulate. You wanted it. Don't try to play me like that."** Chanel tried to move past him. Still no success. "Can you please move over so I can get into my condo please?"

"Why so you can run away from me again," he demanded.

"Trey, I don't have the time. Can you please me? I asked you nicely." **"OKAY, YOUR POINT."** Chanel got so fed up she pushed her way past Trey.

"Damn, like that?" he barked as he walked behind her.

"Please move back! Do not get that close to me."

"Or what?" he demanded.

"Or this!" Chanel grabbed the mace in her purse and maced Trey in his face and mouth. He started screaming at the top of his lungs. She hurried into her apartment and grabbed as much as she could. Trey, who was still screaming in the hallway, alerted the other neighbors. Everyone came into the hallway to find out what all the commotion was about. Chanel just focused on getting new clothes. She packed her bag as best as she could. As she headed out the door, Trey, who managed to stand to his feet, was blocking the door.

"You b****," he yelled. Chanel smiled and said, "you deserve it." She pushed Trey, and he fell into another neighbor. Chanel hurried to her car and drove off as fast as she could. She was so focused on the road that she didn't hear her phone ring. Chanel was nervous. She couldn't believe what just happened. *Oh, my God.* When she arrived at her doctor's appointment, she rushed inside the building. The time was 1:15. *Shoot.* Chanel frantically signed in and took a seat in the waiting room. She looked down at her phone and saw she had a missed call. It was from a number she didn't recognize. However, the number left a message. Chanel clicked the voicemail, and it was the man. The statement reads: "Hey Chanel, it's Tony from Brother Properties and Equities. You and your friend came looking for a way to move out of your current condominium and into another complex altogether. After much conversation, we have decided to transfer to our Parkway Chase condominiums in the downtown area. I know you wanted to be close to your school, but I think it would better fit for you. Plus, you will be close to your friend. When you get this message, please call me back." Chanel started crying in the waiting room. *"Thank you, God! Thank you, God!"* Everything was working out in her favor. Just then, Dr. Smith, her psychologist, emerged from around the corner.

"Chanel," she said. Chanel looked up, and her psychologist could see that she was crying. She immediately sat next to her.

"Is everything okay?"

Chanel answered her with the biggest smile on her face, "everything is just fine."

ABOUT THE AUTHOR

Marche' is an eccentric woman who loves God and a wonderful mother to her daughter Semira. They live together in their small home, complete with a dog, cat, and two birds. When she's not writing, she attending school part-time, a blogger, and teaches nutrition to those in low-income communities.

CPSIA information can be obtained
at www.ICGtesting.com
Printed in the USA
LVHW092022040122
707795LV00001B/13

9 781643 147048